FROM GOD'S
HEART TO MINE

FROM GOD'S HEART TO MINE

• LEARNING SCRIPTURE BY GOD'S LOVING TOUCH •

DR. DIANE M. BOLL

© 2010 by Diane M. Boll. All rights reserved.
2nd Printing 2014

Trusted Books is an imprint of Deep River Books. The views expressed or implied in this work are those of the author. To learn more about Deep River Books, go online to www.DeepRiverBooks.com.

No part of this publication may be reproduced, stored in a retrieval system, or transmitted in any way by any means—electronic, mechanical, photocopy, recording, or otherwise—without the prior permission of the publisher, except as provided by USA copyright law.

Unless otherwise noted, all Scriptures are taken from the *Holy Bible, New International Version®, NIV*. Copyright © 1973, 1978, 1984 by Biblica, Inc.™ Used by permission of Zondervan. All rights reserved worldwide. www.zondervan.com

Scripture references marked NASB are taken from the *New American Standard Bible*, © 1960, 1963, 1968, 1971, 1972, 1973, 1975, 1977 by The Lockman Foundation. Used by permission.

ISBN 13: 978-1-63269-231-3
Library of Congress Catalog Card Number: 2010902980

CONTENTS

Introduction..vii

God is a Shield of Integrity, Character, and Conviction 1
Born of God...5
Rebellion and Sin...9
Born Again..13
Fear 15
The Critical Voice...19
Forgiveness...23
Rebellion 25
Joy 27
Boundaries...29
Creativity..33
Impatience...35
Responsibility..37
Insecurity..39
A Child Forever 43
Shame/Love/Sex/Marriage 45
Pride Versus Gift from God 49

Death 51
Unconditional Love 53
Dysfunction and Crisis. 55
Burdens 59
Faith. 61
Praise 63
Wisdom and Intuition 65
Anger. 67
Loss 69
Hurt, Healing, and Trust 73
Disappointments 75
Love. 77
Counsel 79
Expectations. 81
Emotions 83
Gender. 87
Confusion 89
Guilty as Judged. 91
Security 95
Maturity. 97
God's Purpose for My Life 101
Change and Sadness. 103
Secrets 107
Failure 111
Lies We Lived/Changing Childlike Perspectives 113
Control 115
Rejection 117

INTRODUCTION

THIS BOOK BEGAN when I was diagnosed with breast cancer. It was a period of reflection and insight into my soul. God took me to the deepest core of myself and brought me to an understanding of how deeply He works. He gave me time to write, and even greater emotional healing during a time when my body needed healing. I felt His consistent presence as never before.

This new understanding motivated me to write these articles of affirmation for the many Christians who come to therapy needing the loving touch of God's Word to heal hurts from the past. These pages are a result of years of reading the Word of God and experiencing personal healing. As I began to apply the principles of God's Word to my personal life, my heart was healed. Having the privilege of working with people in pain, including friends and clients, has helped me understand the pain and emotions that we all must endure in our lifetime. The situations discussed in the following chapters are from clients, friends, and my own experiences. As you read, allow yourself to see the heart of God and allow the words to permeate your soul. I pray that reading God's Word will support healing, just as God's Word helped me.

FROM GOD'S HEART TO MINE

In Matthew 18, Jesus is talking to His disciples. He asks the question, "Who is the greatest in the kingdom of heaven?" In addition, He called a child to Himself and set him before them, and said, "Truly I say to you, unless you are converted and become like children, you will not enter the kingdom of heaven. Whoever then humbles himself as this child, he is the greatest in the kingdom of heaven. And whoever receives one such child in My name receives Me; but whoever causes one of these little ones who believe in Me to stumble, it is better for him that a heavy millstone be hung around his neck, and to be drowned in the depth of the sea" (verses 1-6 NASB).

The above statements reflect the truth of how God made us. He knows people need new beginnings. The child within all of us needs to begin again, too. Children have no problem coming to God humbly and innocently. But the hurts from the past sometimes interfere with an adult's ability to come humbly before God. Critical, neglectful, or abusive parents or adults are our models for how God might treat us. Our unconscious beliefs from childhood can distort our understanding of God, others, and ourselves.

God is the perfect parent and the place where healing can begin. Jesus not only died for our sins and gives us eternal life in heaven, but He also gives us the gifts of forgiveness, love, and peace. He provides the opportunity for a second chance through becoming a child of God. He helps us grow emotionally to eventually be the adult He calls us to be. His emotional peace and guidance will free us to do His work.

When we are born, God gives us parents until we develop the reasoning side of our brain. The problem starts with parents who model dysfunctional patterns and thoughts. As adults we mimic old patterns developed during childhood. When stressful situations arise, the old patterns arise, and unconsciously the emotional child within tends to make the decisions. We often become reactors to situations. We think we are making adult decisions, but we are impulsive and reactive like children. But God can re-parent us with His Word. He develops our intellectual side by helping us acknowledge self-destructive behaviors.

INTRODUCTION

In God's Word, He gives us directions to set a solid foundation of moral character. In the past, our moral character was like shifting sand. When we are disobedient, we may reap temporary gratification, but later we suffer consequences. God's Word helps to set us on the Rock (Christ), who offers forgiveness and grace. God loves us and wants us to feel our feelings and come to Him with them, but if we act on the negative feelings we may sin continuously.

There are times when help from Christian professionals can provide empathy and understanding that paves the way to healing. When adults grasp the truth of God, the hurt child is set free from the pain and distorted perceptions of childhood. I wrote this book to provide a source of direction for healing from God's Word. May God be with you through your healing journey.

GOD IS A SHIELD OF INTEGRITY, CHARACTER, AND CONVICTION

THE SHIELD THAT God builds is within us. The Holy Spirit has come to build strong individuals through the process of sanctification. We are in a process of purification that builds our integrity and character and can result in strong convictions motivating us to help others to have the same experience and relationship with God.

According to the computer Word Perfect program dictionary, *integrity* is "an unreduced or unbroken completeness or moral soundness; adherence to a code of values."

> He who walks with integrity, and works righteousness, and speaks truth in his heart. He does not slander with his tongue, nor does evil to his neighbor, nor takes up a reproach against his friend; in whose eyes a reprobate is despised, but who honors those who fear the LORD; he swears to his own hurt and does not change... He who does these things will never be shaken.
> —Psalm 15:2-5 (NASB)

> The integrity of the upright will guide them, but the crookedness of the treacherous will destroy them... The righteousness of the blameless will smooth his way, but the wicked will fall by his own wickedness.

FROM GOD'S HEART TO MINE

The righteousness of the upright will deliver them, but the treacherous will be caught by their own greed.
—Proverbs 11:3, 5-6 (NASB)

Character is defined as "the inherent attributes that determine a person's moral and ethical actions and reactions; a person of good repute; a characteristic that defines the individual nature of something or someone." *Conviction* is defined as "an unshakeable belief in something without need for proof or evidence."

Integrity is an integral part of healthy emotions and healthy individuals. God's shield protects those who have integrity. Sin fractures and ultimately destroys a person from within. God has such a love for us that He has shown us the righteous path of eternal life with Him and a life of peace here on earth, but we have to grasp the Word and apply it to our lives. We can accept Christ and have eternal life while still continuing to do things our own way and miss the life Christ has for us. Or we can begin to turn our will and lives over to the living God and trust Him to lead us into a life of integrity and peace.

What are the major reasons we lose integrity? Ever remember telling a lie? You might have felt conviction and guilt, and robbed of peace. Then you might have to tell another lie to cover the first. It becomes a slippery slope downward and you feel bad about yourself. It is easier to lie the next time because it becomes a pattern, a feeling that you are protecting yourself.

A lack of integrity is a slow process that can take years to develop. It might start with a lie to get out of trouble, or you may fear losing a friendship, or lying could be a way to manipulate situations and circumstances for your own benefit. Exaggeration, too, is a lie that seeks attention from others. Soon you are lying, cheating, or stealing. It erodes your self-esteem and you now can't let anyone too close or they might see the truth. Sin sears the heart and you soon become hardened. Sin separates you from close relationship with others and with God. The erosion begins with feelings of guilt and shame that may make you feel less lovable and less able to love others. We feel we are less capable of taking care of ourselves.

GOD IS A SHIELD OF INTEGRITY, CHARACTER, AND CONVICTION

Guilt can be a good thing because it is the first sign we need to change something. The world wants to rid itself of guilt by saying everything is okay, there is no sin. This logic does not work, because sin in itself is destructive. Guilt is God's way of protecting our integrity, our character, and us. God is the shield. He takes away our guilt through forgiveness because of His death on the cross. Then He sent the Holy Spirit to support our self-esteem with integrity and character so that we might have conviction that changes the heart. Conviction says, I will not cheat, steal, lie, do drugs, commit adultery, etc.

Conviction is non-negotiable. It begins with trusting God, submitting, and building a relationship, knowing that when you are tempted He will provide a way out. Whenever you fail, ask for forgiveness, pray for help, and change will come in time. Change does not necessarily come automatically. God may want you to work at it by allowing you to experience situations where you must make choices but He promises He will always give you a way out.

> No temptation has overtaken you but such as is common to man; and God is faithful, who will not allow you to be tempted beyond what you are able, but with the temptation will provide the way of escape also, so that you will be able to endure it.
> —1 Corinthians: 10:13 (NASB)

What kind of moral integrity and character do you have? Where might you improve? Who do you want to be as a human being, in Christ?

Journal your feelings about integrity, character, and conviction.

_____
_____
_____
_____

BORN OF GOD

GOD GIVES US the hope of a new life. Each New Year we reflect on the past and set goals for the future. There is hope in new beginnings in Christ Jesus.

> Yet to all who received him, to those who believed in his name, he gave the right to become children of God—children born not of natural descent, nor of human decision or a husband's will, but born of God.
> —John 1:12-13

> So also, when we were children, we were in slavery under the basic principles of the world. But when the time had fully come, God sent his Son, born of a woman, born under law, to redeem those under law, that we might receive the full rights of sons. Because you are sons, God sent the Spirit of his Son into our hearts, the Spirit who calls out, 'Abba, Father.' (Here, Abba means DADDY!)
> —Galatians 4:3-6

> Those who are led by the Spirit of God are sons of God. For you did not receive a spirit that makes you a slave again to fear, but you

received the Spirit of sonship. And by him we cry, 'Abba, Father.' The Spirit himself testifies with our spirit that we are God's children.
—Romans 8:14-16

You are all sons of God through faith in Christ Jesus.
—Galatians 3:26

Believing that Christ died for your sins, knowing you are a sinner, asking for forgiveness, and asking Christ into your heart are the keys to becoming a child of God. You know when you truly believe and you then become a child of God.

Because we are born again, we are new babies who can be molded into the children God intended us to be. We were previously molded into our dysfunctional family's ways. We reacted to whatever happened in our lives. Hurt permeated our soul. When those in authority hurt us, it became difficult to listen because of the emotional pain. In our dysfunctional homes, feelings were not allowed and telling the truth could result in being ridiculed. Trying to make others happy was a way to keep peace in the home. Other times, seeking pleasure with things such as using alcohol, drugs, sex, or pornography became a way to cover up feelings. The heart began to freeze up when life became overwhelmingly painful. Keeping others at a distance kept loneliness in full bloom. The heart could not accept the love of God or love from anyone else. The desire for happiness and pleasure caused both immediate pleasure, and then later suffering painful consequences. Not knowing what was healthy, the family's dysfunction permeated every part of life.

Today, God is in the process of supporting our emotional health. God is not looking for perfection, just progress. God can work with us as we yield. We begin to understand that we can't control people, places, or things. Only God is in control and He gives us free will to make mistakes or obey. Acknowledging we are sinful and receiving forgiveness is the first step to our new life. Learning from mistakes is important because

BORN OF GOD

it is the only way to grow. Knowing each day is a new day, we can focus on the forgiveness of Christ and what He has done and the hope He offers for all for eternity; we can experience a changed life today. Today is a new life, a new beginning in Christ. Christ came at just the right time and died for you and me.

Journal about the hurt and anger.
Journal about your hope for a new life.

_____
_____
_____
_____
_____
_____
_____
_____
_____
_____
_____
_____
_____
_____
_____
_____
_____
_____

REBELLION AND SIN

ALL HAVE SINNED and fallen short of the glory of God. If we say we have not sinned, we are lying to ourselves. God can't redeem us when we are in denial. Rebellion is a natural instinct and one response to hurt. A child in rebellion is reacting to a real or perceived painful world. Everyone wants to feel loved and we often fear that things will never change. Looking for love can lead to sin. Today, we are learning that God does not want us to be reactors to pain. He wants us to be proactive by learning a different response. He desires us to cast all our cares on Him. We do not have to sin when confronted with painful situations. No matter what situation we come from, it's never okay to sin. It only hurts others and us. Sin can develop into a cycle that causes us hurt, to get angry, and to hurt others. We then feel bad about ourselves and unconsciously blame others, but never resolve the real issues of personal pain. Anger and rebellion can become an excuse to do wrong, which keeps us in bondage. Today we are set free to choose to no longer be a slave to the sinful nature.

> Don't you know that when you offer yourselves to someone to obey him as slaves, you are slaves to the one whom you obey—whether

you are slaves to sin, which leads to death, or to obedience, which leads to righteousness? But thanks be to God that, though you used to be slaves to sin, you wholeheartedly obeyed the form of teaching to which you were entrusted. You have been set free from sin and have become slaves to righteousness.

I put this in human terms because you are weak in your natural selves. Just as you used to offer the parts of your body in slavery to impurity and to ever-increasing wickedness, so now offer them in slavery to righteousness leading to holiness… But now that you have been set free from sin and have become slaves to God, the benefit you reap leads to holiness, and the result is eternal life. For the wages of sin is death, but the gift of God is eternal life in Christ Jesus our Lord.
—Romans 6:16-19, 22-23

For you did not receive a spirit that makes you a slave again to fear, but you received the Spirit of sonship. And by him we cry 'ABBA (daddy), Father.' (You are a child of God.)
—Romans 8:15

For I am convinced that neither death, nor life, nor angels, nor principalities, nor things present, nor things to come, nor powers, [39] nor height, nor depth, nor any other created thing, will be able to separate us from the love of God, which is in Christ Jesus our Lord.
—Roman 8:38-39 (NASB)

Today, we can practice taking one day at a time, knowing that God loves the sinner, not the sin. We can reflect on what He did for us on the cross and open our hearts to receive His love. Choices today can reflect the way Christ loves us. God is a healthy, balanced Father who loves and sets limits to keep us safe. Therefore, the adult inside can learn to listen to God's guidance. As Christ forgives us, we can learn to forgive others and ourselves. In the same way, we can learn to love others and the child

REBELLION AND SIN

within. God's Word is alive and active and it can provide healing. God never takes His love away. We are the ones who turn our backs to God. Comprehending how much He loves us can be difficult, but through Christ we can do all things through Him who strengthens us.

Today we no longer have to rebel. We have direct access to God. We can pray and discuss the right way to do things when we disagree with others. If we have faith the size of a mustard seed, God can create new hearts in us. He says He will redeem what the locust has destroyed. We do not do this; rather Christ and the Spirit in us, as we yield to Him daily. Thank You, Lord, for the blessings we have been given. Amen.

Journal about what you have learned in these passages.

_____
_____
_____
_____
_____
_____
_____
_____
_____
_____
_____
_____
_____
_____
_____
_____

BORN AGAIN

Jesus declared, 'I tell you the truth, no one can see the kingdom of God unless he is born again.'
—John 3:3

For God so loved the world that he gave his one and only Son, that whoever believes in him shall not perish but have eternal life. (17) For God did not send his Son into the world to condemn the world, but to save the world through him.
—John 3:16-17

TODAY WE KNOW we are sinners who were destined for destruction and death. We have asked Christ to forgive us. We believe that He is the Christ, the Son of the living God, who died on the cross for our sins, and we now have a new, abundant life. He has cleansed us from all sin. We are free and no longer in bondage to sin. We can now choose to sin or not. As we turn our lives over to Him, daily we can live righteously without the condemnation of sin. We are babes in Christ, a new creation.

Memories of past childhood disappointments, neglect, and abuses can destroy the joy and blessing God has for us today. Because we are infants in Christ, understanding how to take care of infants is important.

FROM GOD'S HEART TO MINE

Infants need milk, sleep, and love to grow physically, emotionally, and spiritually. Resting and feeding on God's Word because it is the bread of life is important for our growth. Crying when we are uncomfortable is part of growing in Christ because we can now feel the pain and losses from the past. We can bathe in Christ's love and care as He meets our needs. We can grow and reach out and fully engage the world, even as we are released from having to be like the world. As we mature in Christ, we can rest in His love, forgiveness, and grace. Because of what He did on the Cross, we no longer have to feel shame.

Today, we can reach out to others and receive nurturing and love. We can love God, love others, and love ourselves. We no longer need to withdraw and isolate or use risky or destructive behaviors to cope with pain. We can rely on God's Word and the Holy Spirit to guide us. We can learn to be a loving parent to the precious infant inside. We are set free from the past abuse to live in Christ. We are no longer victims, but victors in Christ.

Thank You, Lord.

Journal how you are achieving victory over a painful past and the hope of a new life.

_____

_____

_____

_____

_____

_____

_____

FEAR

WHEN CHILDREN ARE young, they often experience night terrors. Children worry about monsters, burglars, or crawly things. At nighttime, the darkness seems to hold endless terror. As adults, we know that when we were children we were hurt by others or might not have received sufficient protection from other adults. Sometimes the adults who were supposed to protect us hurt us. Fear, oppression, and terror go together. Oppression keeps us from becoming all God made us to be. Fear and oppression keep us from taking responsibility to do what God wants us to do. Terror paralyzes us and we withdraw and hide. God has not given us the spirit of fear; the truth found in the Word of God sets us free.

Today, we can embrace the fear in the darkness. The imagination might be full of fear, but really things in the mind can't hurt us. Fear can shrink our world when we withdraw to what we believe is safety, but doing so keeps us lonely. Today, we can keep safe by making good choices based on the Word of God. We can now learn to embrace feelings even though they are not always truthful, and we can let go of the lies we often believed as children. Granted, they are our feelings, but scaring ourselves does not change anything—worry just causes anxiety. We can now have the peace of Christ because He sent the Holy Spirit to guide us into all truth. We can let go and let God take over the things we have no control over. We can live in the present and enjoy this day. It's not easy to stop worrying about things that may never happen. Listening to the conversations in our heads and how we scare ourselves is a start. There are three types of fears most people worry about: fear of death; fear of rejection; fear of failure "What if the plane crashes?" "What will people think of me?" " What if I fail or can't do it?" These are conversations most people dwell on. God has much to say about worry and fear.

> Be anxious for nothing, but in everything by prayer and supplication with thanksgiving let your requests be made known to God. [7] And the peace of God, which surpasses all comprehension, will guard your hearts and your minds in Christ Jesus. [8] Finally, brethren, whatever is true, whatever is honorable, whatever is right, whatever is pure, whatever is lovely, whatever is of good repute, if there is any excellence and if anything worthy of praise, let your mind dwell on these things.
>
> —Philippians 4:6-8 (NASB)

> In my anguish I cried to the LORD, and he answered by setting me free. The LORD is with me; I will not be afraid. What can man do to me? The LORD is with me; he is my helper. I will look in triumph on my enemies. It is better to take refuge in the LORD than to trust in man. It is better to take refuge in the LORD than to trust in princes.
>
> —Psalm 118:5-9

Today is a new day. As adults, we can take care of matters because we have more resources and greater understanding of the Word, of the world, and of life. We now can trust God to carry us through whatever we have to go through. We can make choices that are based on knowledge and truth, instead of fear and anxiety. We can ask God to help us through a prayer such as: " God grant me the serenity to accept the things I can not change, the courage to change the things I can and the wisdom to know the difference." (Serenity Prayer of AA)

We can rely on the Word of God and the Holy Spirit's help to change our imagination from fear to peace. We can make positive choices to relax the mind and body. Understanding the distorted perceptions we have of God, others, and ourselves, we can work to keep the truth before us so that we don't fall back into old patterns.

> 'In righteousness you will be established; you will be far from oppression, for you will not fear; and from terror, for it will not come near you. (15) If anyone fiercely assails you it will not be from Me… No weapon that is formed against you will prosper; and every tongue that accuses you in judgment you will condemn. This is the heritage of the servants of the Lord, and their vindication is from Me,' declares the Lord.
> —Isaiah 54:14-15, 17 (NASB)

> The Lord is my light and my salvation—whom shall I fear? The Lord is the stronghold of my life—of whom shall I be afraid?
> —Psalm 27:1

> For God has not given us a spirit of timidity (fear), but a spirit of power, and love and of self-discipline (or sound mind).
> —2 Timothy 1:7

> But when he, the Spirit of truth, comes, he will guide you into all truth.
> —John 16:13

FROM GOD'S HEART TO MINE

Journal about how the past situations are still impacting your decision-making today.

Ask God to come into all the painful situations from the past and heal the wounds and comfort you in the fearful situations from the past.

> God of all comfort; who comforts us in all our affliction so that we may be able to comfort those who are in any affliction with the comfort with which we ourselves are comforted by God.
> —2 Corinthians 1:3b-4

_____
_____
_____
_____
_____
_____
_____
_____
_____
_____
_____
_____
_____
_____
_____

THE CRITICAL VOICE

THE CRITICAL VOICE in our heads comes from critical parents, caregivers, or siblings. The voices play like a recorder in our minds, playing over and over. Because we have minds like computers that record every word, we no longer need others to criticize us; our own critical voice plays old tapes that continue to hurt us. The past criticism prevents us from accepting constructive criticism. The child in us transforms any comment into a personal attack such as, "You're stupid, ugly; you are never good enough." We can silence the old negative messages and replace them with healthy thoughts such as, "No, that is a lie. I am intelligent, beautiful, and am capable of doing wonderful things."

Before Christ came into our hearts, the child inside heard the negative comments and became very angry. Walls went up. Nothing is allowed in when we're angry. Our natural response is to yell back, get even, or withdraw. When we keep our walls up we can't receive love from God, others, or ourselves. The walls feel good for a while because we feel safe, but we soon begin to feel that no one cares, which makes us feel lonely.

God created us to need one another. Today, we can silence the old negative messages and replace them with healthy thoughts. We can assess our anger. Am I hurt or irritated at others because I am depressed or sad? Am I pushing others away because I am overwhelmed? Am I exaggerating the situation because of my past? Negative lies about others and ourselves can drain our energy or set us up for loneliness.

> 'In your anger do not sin': Do not let the sun go down while you are still angry, and do not give the devil a foothold.
> —Ephesians 4:26-27

> For man's anger does not bring about the righteous life that God desires. Therefore, get rid of all moral filth and the evil that is so prevalent and humbly accept the Word planted in you, which can save you. Do not merely listen to the Word, and so deceive yourselves. Do what it says.
> —James 1:20-22

> Be anxious for nothing, but in everything by prayer and supplication with thanksgiving let your requests be made known to God. And the peace of God, which surpasses all comprehension, will guard your hearts and your minds in Christ Jesus. Finally, brethren, whatever is true, whatever is honorable, whatever is right, whatever is pure, whatever is lovely, whatever is of good repute, if there is any excellence, and if anything worthy of praise, dwell on these things.
> —Philippians 4:6-8 (NASB)

Today, we can use self-talk for positive change and silence the negatives that have no bearing on our lives. We can learn to talk to the child within with respect, love, and care. We say instead, "I am God's creation and wonderfully made. I am a child of God who is lovable, capable, and competent." Because we are no longer critical of ourselves, we are better able to receive constructive criticism without becoming defensive. We can take time to look inside and process whether our behavior needs to change.

THE CRITICAL VOICE

We can now change negative attitudes into positive behaviors that reflect the true child of God. We can accept the love that God and others offer. We can feel a part of God's family today.

> Are not two sparrows sold for a penny? Yet not one of them will fall to the ground apart from the will of your Father. And even the very hairs of your head are all numbered. So don't be afraid; you are worth more than many sparrows.
> —Matthew 10:29-31

Journal about the things that make you angry. Ask the Holy Spirit to reveal where the root of the anger came from. God knows and understands. He knows all the tears you have shed and knows how many hairs are on your head.

_____
_____
_____
_____
_____
_____
_____
_____
_____
_____
_____
_____
_____
_____
_____

FORGIVENESS

THIS IS THE day of new beginnings. Christ has forgiven us. As children, there comes a time when we begin to realize the world is not all good. We realize friends can be mean. We recognize there are family and friends who do not care about us. Others let us down. We try very hard to be good but others might not care for us as much as we care for them. The realization that we are not all that important to others hurts. Our self-esteem is injured, and our self-confidence is diminished. Loss, broken promises, and experiences in life can break the heart of the trusting innocence of the child within.

Today, we can begin to forgive others who have hurt us. We can forgive ourselves for hurting others. We can become trustworthy and learn to trust those who are trustworthy. Today, we understand:

- Trustworthy people do not lie.
- Trustworthy people work on their own issues.
- Trustworthy people take responsibility for their actions.
- Trustworthy people apologize and change their behavior.
- Trustworthy people can accept constructive criticism without blowing up.

FROM GOD'S HEART TO MINE

Today, we will not allow the past to rob us of all the blessings that God has for us. We can embrace forgiveness, knowing how much Christ loves us. God's love heals the losses and hurts from the past. We can choose to grasp God's promises as our own.

> But now you must rid yourselves of all such things as these: anger, rage, malice, slander, and filthy language from your lips. Do not lie to each other, since you have taken off your old self with its practices and have put on the new self, which is being renewed in knowledge in the image of its Creator. Here there is no Greek or Jew, circumcised or uncircumcised, barbarian, Scythian, slave or free, but Christ is all, and is in all. Therefore, as God's chosen people, holy and dearly loved, clothe yourselves with compassion, kindness, humility, gentleness and patience. Bear with each other and forgive whatever grievances you may have against one another. Forgive as the Lord forgave you.
> —Colossians 3:8-13

> 'I have loved you with an everlasting love; I have drawn you with loving-kindness. I will build you up again and you will be rebuilt.'
> —Jeremiah 31:3-4

Journal your hurts and how Christ has or can make a change in your heart today.

_____
_____
_____
_____
_____
_____
_____

REBELLION

WHEN WE BECOME teenagers we realize we can make our own choices. In rebellion, we feel like doing the opposite of what people in authority would want. We can become tired of being told what to do. We hear too often commands like, "Clean up your room!" "Do the dishes!" "Stop making messes!" We are okay with a sloppy room and we think, "What's the problem? Just get off my back."

Today, the rebellious teenager within can still control our thoughts. We can have conflicting conversations in our heads. "I know I shouldn't buy that, but I deserve it, even if I can't afford it." "I want that cheeseburger even if I am gaining weight." "I hate cleaning because no one helps or cares to keep things clean." "Why do I have to clean; I'm busy, you can do it." "On the other hand, when things are a mess, I get overwhelmed and it causes me more stress." As teens, we really were afraid of the future. We procrastinate in taking responsibility for our own life; we put off things until the last minute. It's easier to get angry with others and act like a mule because the reward is doing nothing. God knows how obstinate we have been; pursuing only the things we want to do. Sometimes we created chaos because we were just bored. It often took us down roads we really didn't want to travel. Today, we can learn to be comfortable without chaos and learn to be comfortable in our own skin.

As adults, we can take care of household tasks and enjoy when the house is clean. When we finish using something, we can choose to clean it and put it away. We work *with* ourselves instead of rebelling. We can learn to enjoy win/win situations for others and ourselves. We can enjoy the clean restful environment we have created for ourselves. Our home and our lives can now be a reflection of the new inner peace that God's grace and forgiveness has given. We can now build our lives on the solid rock of Jesus.

> Therefore everyone who hears these words of mine and puts them into practice is like a wise man who built his house on the rock. The rain came down, the streams rose, and the winds blew and beat against that house; yet it did not fall, because it had its foundation on the rock.
> —Matthew 7:24-25

There is forgiveness and peace when we build our lives on the rock.

> The Lord our God is merciful and forgiving, even though we have rebelled against him.
> —Daniel 9:9

> All day long I have held out my hands to an obstinate people who walk in ways not good, pursuing their own imaginations.
> —Isaiah 65:2

> Peace I leave with you; my peace I give you. I do not give to you as the world gives. Do not let your hearts be troubled and do not be afraid.
> —John 14:27

Journal about what causes your rebellion.

_____

_____

_____

JOY

Praise be to the Lord for he has heard my cry for mercy.
—Psalm 28:6

Then they cried to the Lord in their trouble, and he saved them from their distress. He sent forth his word and healed them; he rescued them from the grave. Let them give thanks to the Lord for his unfailing love and his wonderful deeds for men.
—Psalm 107:19-21

In God, whose word I praise, in the Lord, whose word I praise, in God I trust; I will not be afraid. What can man do to me? I am under vows to you, O God; I will present my thank offerings to you. For you have delivered me from death and my feet from stumbling, that I may walk before God in the light of life.
—Psalm 56:10-13

WE CAN GIVE thanks to the Lord, who heals us through His Word. We can sing a new song. Children love to sing and dance. God has given us joy and today we can sing without the critical inner voice. As a child we might have dreamt of singing on stage or in a group.

FROM GOD'S HEART TO MINE

But we felt too self-conscious. We thought we needed to be perfect in all things. We believed we needed to do many things perfectly in order to gain approval and love. Sometimes we would just give up. Today, we can be okay; we don't have to be perfect. We can like who we are. We don't have to sing like a professional. It feels good deep in the soul to sing a song to the Lord, thanking Him because of all the changes in our lives. It has not been easy giving up perfection. Today we understand we are a work in progress and God is faithful to continue to do a good work in us.

Journal about your progress.

_____
_____
_____
_____
_____
_____
_____
_____
_____
_____
_____
_____
_____

BOUNDARIES

GOD SET BOUNDARIES for us. He separated the dark from the light, water from the earth. God made the wondrous world and all that is in it. He knows what we need. We need boundaries. God gave us the law to set boundaries between right and wrong—otherwise we get out of control. Boundaries help us take responsibility for our own actions. God supports us when we set healthy boundaries such as moral convictions not to steal, cheat, lie, commit adultery, etc. Boundaries help us take responsibility for our own actions and not blame others for how we feel and act out. We should not condemn ourselves but feel the guilt using it to change our sinful behavior, while keeping mindful that we are a work in progress.

God gave us freedom to choose not to sin. He broke the chains of sin so we might be slaves to righteousness. But where are the boundaries in relationships or friendships? It's okay to say no when you become overwhelmed with too much to do. It's okay to take time to sit with God and hear what is right for *your* life, regardless of what others think. We are to look to God for direction, not to people. When we were young we needed others to accept us to feel good about ourselves. Today, we know Jesus accepts us, so we can then accept ourselves.

FROM GOD'S HEART TO MINE

We have the right to our own feelings, thoughts, and opinions based on what is right according to God's Word. God's rules are boundaries that help keep others and yourself safe.

In dysfunctional homes, there are boundaries, but they are only adhered to when it is convenient. Parents are supposed to help set boundaries for their children so they can learn and explore in a safe environment. When we were young, we would explore on our own, and when we went too far, we were criticized or hit. We only found out the boundaries after we crossed them. The boundaries were never explained beforehand. As a result, we began to see ourselves as bad. As a child, we learned the world was an unsafe place. We would isolate at times to keep safe. Sometimes, we would do the opposite of keeping safe, just to rebel against the neglectful or harsh treatment. We could not enjoy the adventure of exploration within boundaries. We also allowed others to invade personal boundaries. Today, we know what we believe, and we are able to say "no" when something goes against our beliefs, feelings, or desires. It is okay to say "no" when we are tired and not feel guilty. It is okay to say "no" when others want us to go against what we believe. We can set our own boundaries. Boundaries keep us safe.

> When the Most High gave the nations their inheritance, when he divided all mankind, he set up boundaries for the peoples according to the number of the sons of Israel.
> —Deuteronomy 32:8

> It was you who set all the boundaries of the earth; you made both summer and winter.
> —Psalm 74:17

BOUNDARIES

Journal a time when you couldn't say "no" and you were hurt or overwhelmed.

Journal a time when you were able to say "no" and it kept you safe.

Thank God for His Word, which gives us boundaries.

_____
_____
_____
_____
_____
_____
_____
_____
_____
_____
_____
_____
_____
_____
_____
_____
_____
_____
_____

CREATIVITY

In the beginning God created the heavens and the earth... And God said, 'Let the water under the sky be gathered to one place, and let dry ground appear.' And it was so. God called the dry ground 'land,' and the gathered waters he called 'seas.' And God saw that it was good. Then God said, 'Let the land produce vegetation; seed bearing plants and trees on the land that bear fruit with seed in it, according to their various kinds.' And it was so.

—Genesis 1:1, 9-11

GOD IS CREATIVE. He made us in His image. We have a creative side that God gave us. Creativity begins with exploration.

When we were children, we needed to explore the wonders of God's creation. We needed to feel the mud ooze through our fingers and toes. We needed to experience the wind and rain. We loved to stomp in puddles and make footprints in the mud. Parents often could not stand us being messy. Making a mess was bad. We quickly learned to be clean and not make a mess. Being scolded was not fun. We felt like we were bad for getting dirty.

Today, we will allow the child within to go into the garden. We may wear old clothes and get down on our hands and knees. We can love digging into the damp earth and smelling the smells. We can love the idea of planting a seed and watching flowers and vegetables grow. We can feel a part of God when we are planting the seeds. We can feel God's love and care when the earth yields its fruits and vegetables. The world God made is beautiful and He desires for us to enjoy it and take care of it.

Today, we can also begin to explore other creative areas. We can learn to draw, play an instrument, dance, and feel our imagination explore all the possibilities of invention to become all God made us to be. God made us in His image, and He is the ultimate creator.

Journal about the love you feel from God when you look at what He created.

Thank Him for creating you and the world around you.

_____
_____
_____
_____
_____
_____
_____
_____
_____
_____
_____
_____

IMPATIENCE

TODAY, WE CAN feel impatient with our progress. The world is all about immediate gratification. We have fast food and pills to fix all kinds of problems. We don't want to diet because it takes so long; so we'll have an operation instead or just take a pill to stop us from eating. We want a good marriage, but aren't willing to work at it. We want children to behave, so we don't have to go through too much trouble. We want God to take away all the pain—*now*. We love the quick fix, but remember that children do not become adults overnight. We can learn to be patient and allow for progress, not perfection.

God has put into place the process of growth. Sometimes the progress is unseen until challenging experiences arise. We have hope in Christ that He will finish the work He has begun. In the past we used to run to pleasure and away from the pain. The flesh was weak and would take control and get us into trouble. Today, however, we are okay just waiting and being confident in the work that God is doing. Today, we can be okay in our own skin. We can walk daily with God and be satisfied.

We find many examples in the Bible of people who waited. Abraham had to wait until he was eighty years old to have a son, even though God had made a covenant with him that he would be the father of many nations. David had to go through many challenges before he became the king. Joseph was dropped into a well to die, sold into slavery, and thrown in jail as he was being transformed into a great man of God.

> ...but also for us, to whom God will credit righteousness--for us who believe in him who raised Jesus our Lord from the dead.
> —Romans 4:24

> Therefore, since we have been justified through faith, we have peace with God through our Lord Jesus Christ, through whom we have gained access by faith into this grace in which we now stand. And we rejoice in the hope of the glory of God. Not only so, but we also rejoice in our sufferings, because we know that suffering produces perseverance; perseverance, character; and character, hope.
> —Romans 5:1-4

Journal about your impatience and the lack of trust in what the Lord is doing in your life.

_____
_____
_____
_____
_____
_____
_____
_____
_____
_____

RESPONSIBILITY

AS A CHILD, we might have received smothering, controlling love from our dysfunctional family. As a result, we became passively dependent on others to meet our needs. We were often given things without having to work for them. We often felt neglected because we expected others to automatically know what we needed. In response, we became angry because we were constantly being let down by others. They constantly failed to make us happy.

Today, we can take responsibility for meeting our own needs. We no longer feel like a dependent child. We are adults who are able to tell others what we need and we are capable of taking care of ourselves. We can accept love and nurturing from others without being so dependent on them. We will take responsibility for being content with whom we are and the blessings God has given. Today we can have contentment in any situation because we have peace and joy in our hearts that only God can give.

> Therefore, my dear friends, as you have always obeyed—not only in my presence, but now much more in my absence—continue to work

FROM GOD'S HEART TO MINE

out your salvation with fear and trembling, for it is God who works in you to will and to act according to his good purpose.
—Philippians 2:12-13

Journal about your past dependency on others and reflect on your growth as you have taken responsibility for yourself before God.

_____

_____

_____

_____

_____

_____

_____

_____

_____

_____

_____

_____

_____

_____

_____

_____

_____

_____

INSECURITY

JESUS IS OUR Redeemer, the Shepherd who is willing to leave the 99 to save the 1. Jesus is faithful to collect all the broken pieces of our lives. He can reconnect the disconnections and bring them together into one whole person when we are willing. Security is trusting in the process of giving up and allowing Him to enter into those dark places to heal. Willingness to give up the walls causes us to feel vulnerable. We only trust ourselves, but we must learn to trust Jesus with our lives in the present and for eternity.

Wounded children often accept the yoke of the alcoholic or dysfunctional parent. They take on more than a child can handle, not by choice, but out of survival. Security is what children need. When security is threatened, children defend both their own security and the family's security to stabilize their environment and keep safe. Divorce, alcoholism or drugs, abuse, mental illness, chronic illnesses, and financial problems all threaten the security of the family. Children do what it takes to defend security. Children feel overwhelmed, because children are not able to take on such responsibility, but the child inside never gives up trying to keep security. These children lose respect for adults and have difficulty accepting love, nurturing, or advice from others.

God gives children the desire to survive even when life is terrible. The weight of parental sin is a heavy yoke. This is the way adults get their needs met outside of God's principles. The heavy yoke of life's wisdom produces a person who does not know what it is to have rest in the soul. We can't pull ourselves out of this pit we are in.

Man's wisdom is void of God's truth. All we know is our own truth. Wisdom apart from God is futile. As a victim we felt we had no choice but to trust in ourselves because no one else was trustworthy. Our lives were built on shifting sand with little stability. But today, we can build our lives on the rock of Jesus' salvation and the Word of God. He gives us the stability that only God can give.

> But thanks be to God that, though you used to be slaves to sin, you wholeheartedly obeyed the form of teaching to which you were entrusted. You have been set free from sin and have become slaves to righteousness.
>
> —Romans 6:17-18

> I waited patiently for the Lord; he turned to me and heard my cry. He lifted me out of the slimy pit, out of the mud and mire; he set my feet on a rock and gave me a firm place to stand He put a new song in my mouth, a hymn of praise to our God. Many will see and fear and put their trust in the Lord. Blessed is the man who makes the Lord his trust, who does not look to the proud, to those who turn aside to false gods.
>
> —Psalm 40:1-4

> Do not conform any longer to the pattern of this world, but be transformed by the renewing of your mind. Then you will be able to test and approve what God's will is—his good, pleasing and perfect will.
>
> —Romans 12:2

INSECURITY

And we know that in all things God works for the good of those who love him, who have been called according to his purpose.
—Romans 8:28

Today we can let go and trust in God. Jesus is a safe place to land. We can sit in the eye of a hurricane where it is calm and find peace, and we can trust that all things will work for good because we love Jesus and have been called according to His purpose. We are learning that we have security in Christ rather than others or ourselves.

Journal your feelings of insecurities and how you feel about letting go and trusting in God.

_____
_____
_____
_____
_____
_____
_____
_____
_____
_____
_____
_____
_____
_____
_____
_____

A CHILD FOREVER

WHEN WE WERE innocent children, we did not want to grow up because we unconsciously believed it meant annihilating the child inside. We saw adults as always miserable, angry, and tired. We wanted to run as far as we could from becoming an adult. Having fun was a quest. We did not understand that part of us could be an adult and still embrace the child within. We can still have the curiosity, creativity, and spontaneity of a child. We can enjoy the beauty of the world God made without destructive behavior. We can embrace being an adult with good instincts and insight gained from struggling. We are able to recognize in ourselves the adult human being who is capable of making positive choices for our lives. Embracing the journey of growing into all God can make us is exciting. It is exciting to honor God by celebrating the experiences that God allowed us to go through so we might become the adult we are today.

> Then we will no longer be infants, tossed back and forth by the waves, and blown here and there by every wind of teaching and by the cunning and craftiness of men in their deceitful scheming. Instead, speaking

FROM GOD'S HEART TO MINE

the truth in love, we will in all things grow up into him who is the Head, that is, Christ.
—Ephesians 4:14-15

Journal about the struggles and experiences that made you the adult you are today.

_____
_____
_____
_____
_____
_____
_____
_____
_____
_____
_____
_____
_____
_____
_____
_____
_____
_____

SHAME/LOVE/SEX/MARRIAGE

TODAY, WE ARE healing from the shame of abuse others inflicted on us during childhood. In response to the abuse, we felt bad about ourselves. We were a reflection of what others thought we were. Today we realize the truth of who we are. We are a reflection of what we believe about ourselves and who God made us to be. God made women/men that are beautiful/handsome, loving, and nurturing. The messages we received from the world distorted our perceptions of what a woman or a man is. The world's view of love turned our feelings about sex into something dirty, something to be ashamed of. God can change our view back to a healthy perspective.

> Your beauty should not come from outward adornment, such as braided hair and wearing of gold jewelry and fine clothes. Instead, it should be that of your inner self, the unfading beauty of a gentle and quiet spirit, which is of great worth in God's sight... Husbands, in the same way be considerate as you live with your wives, and treat them with respect as the weaker [physically] partner and as heirs with you of the gracious gift of life, so that nothing will hinder your prayers.
> —I Peter 3:3-4, 7

FROM GOD'S HEART TO MINE

Men are to love their wives as Christ loved the church and gave His life for her. Men are to respect their wives and not just use them for sexual pleasure when they have a need. Women are to respect and love their husbands and be considerate of their husband's feelings and needs. Women are to value themselves inwardly, not just outwardly to gain attention from men. When a woman only works on the outside of herself, it causes her to feel as though she's an object to be adorned or idolized. It feels good for a short time, but very empty in the long term. The world uses sex for monetary gain and personal physical pleasure without the desired connection that God intentionally wanted for us. The world uses sex to satisfy its insatiable lusts.

God is the one who created sexuality for marriage and our pleasure. It is a process of bonding in love that should not be broken. When divorce occurs it tears people apart and the families around them. The world takes sex lightly and leaves men and women empty. God created us to bond through the sexual union and become one when you are married under a covenant. The bonding occurs even when you are not married, but research has shown that living together ends up in separation more often than when people get married. A marriage commitment and living a godly life is the glue that can keep couples together for life. Sexual love is a powerful driving force that can be destructive or used to bond a married couple for life. God made it for good, not for evil.

Today, we can learn to embrace the God-given gift of sexuality without fear or shame. We will no longer allow the world's view or perpetrators to have power over how we feel about ourselves. The old tapes from the past are silenced as we embrace the Word of God and understand the truth about sexuality. We love ourselves as God loves us. Therefore, we are able to feel good about our sexuality.

> Let me not be put to shame, O LORD, for I have cried out to you; but let the wicked be put to shame and lie silent in the grave, Let their lying lips be silenced, for with pride and contempt they speak arrogantly against the righteous. How great is your goodness, which

SHAME/LOVE/SEX/MARRIAGE

you have stored up for those who fear you, which you bestow in the sight of men on those who take refuge in you. In the shelter of your presence you hide them from the intrigues of men; in you dwelling you keep them safe from the strife of tongues. Praise be to the LORD for he showed his wonderful love to me when I was in a besieged city… Be strong and take heart, all you who hope in the LORD.
—Psalm 31:17-21, 24

Read Songs of Solomon because it is a beautiful account of sexual love.

Journal your feelings about how God has changed what you believe about sexuality. Think about the differences between the world's view and what is God's view of sex.

_____
_____
_____
_____
_____
_____
_____
_____
_____
_____
_____
_____
_____

PRIDE VERSUS GIFT FROM GOD

PRIDE IS NOT from God. Like a balloon, pride has no substance inside. When we feel empty, have no moral character, feel unloved, or never feel good enough, we must fill up the empty hole with something. God is the one who fills the holes left by lack of morals, neglect, and abuse as a child. We try to fill up the hole inside with things like drugs, alcohol, attention, perfectionism, education, work-a-holism, or religiosity. We unconsciously feel that if we could be good enough, get enough money, gain enough status, buy enough toys, we would finally feel like someone. We see many entertainers and movies stars who end up unfulfilled even as they tried to fill up the empty holes left from childhood. We try to make ourselves feel good, but today we know who we are in Christ. The Creator of the world loves us. We can humble ourselves before God when we make mistakes. We can ask for help to change when we need to. God has given us substance by building positive moral character within us. We can accept forgiveness when we mess up and feel Him at work in our hearts. We know that with God all things are possible. Today, we can trust His Word and the Holy Spirit to support our personal growth.

A man's pride brings him low, but a man of lowly spirit gains honor.
—Proverbs 29:23

FROM GOD'S HEART TO MINE

> And you also were included in Christ when you heard the word of truth, the gospel of your salvation. Having believed, you were marked in him with a seal, the promised Holy Spirit, ¹⁴who is a deposit guaranteeing our inheritance until the redemption of those who are God's possession—to the praise of his glory.
>
> —Ephesians 1:13-14

Journal concerning your pride and God's personal gifts he has given you. Reflect on Christ's love, grace, mercy, and forgiveness.

_____
_____
_____
_____
_____
_____
_____
_____
_____
_____
_____
_____
_____
_____
_____
_____

DEATH

WHEN WE WERE children, we didn't understand what death was; we didn't think about death. As we grew older, we realized that we could die. As teens and young adults we felt invincible and didn't think we would die or get hurt; only others died. At times we might have thought about when we would die and what it would be like, but the thought would be fleeting. We were fearless at times, but later in life we experienced the losses of people we loved and we realized that death was inevitable. We began to worry about what might happen if we died, the family and friends we would miss. Would they miss us? We were unable to enjoy being alive. Today, those of us who are in Christ know we will be in heaven. God gave us a picture of heaven. "Absent from the body, present with the Lord" is the Scripture we can hang onto. Jesus has many mansions and a table waiting for us when we arrive. Today, we can be dead to ourselves and alive in Christ. By accepting our death and our mortality, we are set free. We no longer have to fear death. Christ sets us free, and when he sets us free we are free indeed. We can love God and love others as we love ourselves. We love life because we know we are here for a purpose and God will not take us before He is done with us. We have a lifetime to live that is ordained by God.

FROM GOD'S HEART TO MINE

Now we know that if the earthly tent we live in is destroyed, we have a building from God, an eternal house in heaven, not built by human hands. Meanwhile we groan, longing to be clothed with our heavenly dwelling, because when we are clothed, we will not be found naked. For while we are in this tent, we groan and are burdened, because we do not wish to be unclothed but to be clothed with our heavenly dwelling, so that what is mortal may be swallowed up by life. Now it is God who has made us for this very purpose and has given us the Spirit as a deposit, guaranteeing what is to come. Therefore we are always confident and know that as long as we are at home in the body we are away from the Lord. We live by faith, not by sight. We are confident, I say, and would prefer to be away from the body and at home with the Lord. So we make it our goal to please him, whether we are at home in the body or away from it.
—2 Corinthians 5:1-9

Journal about your fears about dying and how God is changing that perspective. Thank Him for the lifetime He has set before you.

_____
_____
_____
_____
_____
_____
_____
_____
_____
_____

UNCONDITIONAL LOVE

WHEN WE BECOME children of God we are given His unconditional love. We can never feel love deep inside our souls until we feel the love of God. We can grasp moments of deep love, such as when we are given the gift of a wonderful husband, children, or grandchildren. We can understand God's love through these feelings of love, but we have difficulty understanding what the pure love of God is like. God's love is unconditional and we do not have to do anything to earn His love. This is a difficult concept. We don't have to try to be perfect anymore because He will always love His children.

We understand that we are a work in progress rather than perfect, and He is the one growing us up for His purpose. Today, we can make mistakes and not verbally beat ourselves up. In the past, we could never feel love unless we were perfect. At times we would just give up trying.

The problem was that we mixed up love and approval. Love is unconditional, while approval is getting attention for something we have done. We never did things well enough in our child-like perspective. We often felt pushed to achieve more, so we might gain love. We were left feeling, "There is something wrong with me, I can never be good enough."

FROM GOD'S HEART TO MINE

Today, we know our parents loved us in the best way they could. Sometimes they were mean or just self-centered. Some parents neglected their children because of their addictions, but many still had their children's best interest at heart. Parents get overwhelmed with work and get frustrated trying to get their children to obey, perform, or behave. Children do not come with directions.

Today, we don't have to believe there was something wrong with us. We can open up our hearts to little things each day that make us feel loved. Family, friends, beautiful flowers, the sky, a kind word someone might say can be accepted. Most of all we can love ourselves as God loves us. He loves us with all our flaws. We can make mistakes and still be okay with ourselves. We can make a mistake, ask for forgiveness, and learn from each mistake.

> You see, at just the right time, when we were still powerless, Christ died for the ungodly. Very rarely will anyone die for a righteous man, though for a good man someone might possibly dare to die. But God demonstrates his own love for us in this: While we were still sinners, Christ died for us. Since we have now been justified by his blood, how much more shall we be saved from God's wrath through him! For if, when we were God's enemies, we were reconciled to him through the death of his Son, how much more, having been reconciled, shall we be saved through his life! Not only is this so, but we also rejoice in God through our Lord Jesus Christ, through whom we have now received reconciliation.
> —Romans 5:6-11

When we accept Christ we have reconciliation with God through Christ. Journal what His reconciliation means to you and what it's like to be forgiven through His dying for you. Is this real love? Why?

_____

_____

_____

_____

DYSFUNCTION AND CRISIS

AS CHILDREN, WE were in dysfunctional families. We did not choose the family we were born into. We can choose friends, but not family. What is a dysfunctional family? We know today that dysfunctional families do not have clear boundaries. They are comfortable with chaos. Chaos is the only thing they know. The family becomes a collective whole where no one is allowed to be an individual with needs, desires, or opinions of their own. Everyone is made to take care of the security of the family and not cause waves. Problems are covered over and not solved. Pretending and denial become a way of life. Denial is a way of justifying lies. Addictions arise out of the pain of unresolved issues in families.

People make excuses for dysfunction by talking about the crisis in their lives, but crisis does not make a dysfunctional family. Crisis is part of life. Crisis gives God an opportunity to show Himself and His faithfulness. Similarly, it creates an environment where we can begin to trust God's faithfulness. The Bible is full of dysfunction. David was a man after God's own heart, but his family of origin and his married life were full of dysfunction. Abraham made many mistakes in his dysfunctional family life. God redeems peoples' lives when they are able to understand they are sinners.

Addictions, obsessions, compulsions, depression, and anxiety all come from unresolved relationship or family issues. The Bible says, "The sins of the fathers go down three and four generations," so understanding the family sins and the truth can set you free to allow the Holy Spirit to come in and heal the hurts. Jesus can't redeem what the locust has destroyed until the devastation is assessed and the truth is revealed. He can't deliver a person from the pain when they are in denial. Intimacy and truth with God sets you free and solves the problem of loneliness, abandonment, low self-esteem, guilt, shame, etc.

> He heals the brokenhearted, and binds up their wounds. He counts the number of the stars; He gives names to all of them. Great is our Lord and abundant in strength; His understanding is infinite. The LORD supports the afflicted; He brings down the wicked to the ground.
> —Psalm 147:3-6 (NASB)

> For the grace of God has appeared, bringing salvation to all men, instructing us to deny ungodliness and worldly desires and to live sensibly, righteously and godly in the present age, looking for the blessed hope and the appearing of the glory of our great God and Savior, Christ Jesus, who gave Himself for us to redeem us from every lawless deed, and to purify for Himself a people for His own possession, zealous for good deeds. These things speak and exhort and reprove with all authority. Let no one disregard you.
> —Titus 2:11-15 (NASB)

Today, we can choose to live in the truth and look at the family dysfunction, not to blame, but to resolve the pain with God's help. He redeemed our lives to give us eternity with Him in heaven and gave us a great purpose here, as we are zealous to do good deeds. If we are doing good deeds, we won't have time to do lawless deeds. As a result,

DYSFUNCTION AND CRISIS

we are able to give God all the glory for what He has done in us and through us.

Journal what you learned about dysfunctional families and your own family.

BURDENS

AS CHILDREN, WE needed help from our parents to understand the world and how it works. Parents are there to teach us how to function in our world. In the right atmosphere, children love learning to eat on their own, going to the bathroom on their own, helping around the house.

However, our parents often gave us mixed messages. When we asked for help, they would often say, "don't bother me." We began to feel we were bad for asking for help. If we asked for help, we might have to pay a price. We learned to live without our needs met and often had to take care of their needs. We felt deprived or overwhelmed because it became stressful taking care of others and ourselves. Today, when we feel deprived or overwhelmed, we can respond attentively to our own needs. We are adults with multiple resources. As adults, we have capabilities that children do not have. Today, we can choose to pray and cast all our cares on God. We can let go and let God take over to direct our paths.

Today, we can happily respond to our inner child's needs. We are able to ask for help when needed. We are able to respond or not respond to other people's needs without feeling guilty. We realize we can respond to those needs without guilt driving us to feel obligated. We are free to choose. Today, we are set free to give and receive gifts and blessings from God and others.

> Come to Me, all who are weary and heavy-laden, and I will give you rest. Take My yoke upon you and learn from Me, for I am gentle and humble in heart; and you will find rest for your souls. For My yoke is easy and My burden is light.
> —Matthew 11:28-30 (NASB)

Journal about your burdens. Pray and ask God for help in giving your burdens to Him. Ask for strength to do what you can't do alone.

_____
_____
_____
_____
_____
_____
_____
_____
_____
_____
_____
_____
_____
_____
_____

FAITH

If we are faithless, He remains faithful, for He can't deny Himself…
Nevertheless, the firm foundation of God stands, having this seal,
'The Lord knows those who are His.'
> —2 Timothy 2:13, 19 (NASB)

For all have sinned and fall short of the glory of God, being justified as a gift by His grace through the redemption which is in Christ Jesus; whom God displayed publicly as a propitiation in His blood through faith…Where then is boasting? It is excluded. By what kind of law? Of works? No, but by a law of faith. For we maintain that a man is justified by faith apart from works of the Law.
> —Romans 3:23-25, 27-28 (NASB)

WE ARE NOT justified by how good we are, but by faith in Christ. It is what He has done for us, not how good we can be.

One of the major hurdles in recovery has been to overcome the negative programming from childhood. For some children our homes can be full of catastrophe, dysfunction, and chaos. We can grow up expecting things will turn out badly and nothing will ever change.

FROM GOD'S HEART TO MINE

Part of recovery is to discard our expectations of catastrophe and replace them with God's expectations and plans for our life.

> 'For I know the plans that I have for you,' declares the Lord, 'plans for welfare and not for calamity to give you a future and a hope. Then you will call upon Me and come and pray to Me, and I will listen to you. And you will seek Me and find Me when you search for Me with all your heart.'
> —Jeremiah 29:11-13 (NASB)

> And we know that in all things God works for the good of those who love him, who have been called according to his purpose… No, in all these things we are more than conquerors through him who loved us. For I am convinced that neither death nor life, neither angels nor demons, neither the present nor the future, nor any powers, neither height nor depth, nor anything else in all creation, will be able to separate us from the love of God that is in Christ Jesus our Lord.
> —Romans 8:28, 37-39

Today, when situations happen beyond our control, we know that Scripture says God works everything together for good for those who love Him, who have been called according to His purpose. Therefore, we can have confidence that God will direct our path or keep us safe in His arms. He can give us peace in the middle of storms as we keep our eyes focused on Him. We can reflect on how God has brought us out of many catastrophes to make us the strong persons we are today. Today, we can move forward in faith with peace and joy knowing God has us in His hands.

Journal about your faith in Christ.

_____

_____

_____

PRAISE

AS CHILDREN, WE were punished for simply being children. We loved to explore and investigate, but we were made to feel bad, stupid, forgetful, or lazy. We never felt good enough or never seemed to get better. After a while, we no longer needed anyone to say those words—we could blame ourselves for anything that didn't go right.

We became starved for praise, never realizing that praise could be used to manipulate, and we fell for sweet talk, even when it was not truthful. Sweet talk can be used to get something the person wants. Sweet talk leaves us empty. Today, we can learn from past mistakes and discern when we are being manipulated. We don't need sweet talk; we can appreciate the abilities that God gave us. God doesn't make "junk." We can be supportive and encouraging to ourselves like we have been to others. With praise for the good things we do, we can now look at our negative behaviors and apply the grace of God with understanding. We can speak gently and lovingly to our inner child to encourage positive changes, knowing we are forgiven for all our mistakes. Today, we can praise God for the challenges. We can take constructive action instead of choosing destructive behaviors. We know who we are in Christ and have faith He is there to help re-parent and direct our path to become the person He designed.

> But you are a chosen people, a royal priesthood, a holy nation, a people belonging to God, that you may declare the praises of him who called you out of darkness into his wonderful light. Once you were not a people, but now you are the people of God; once you had not received mercy, but now you have received mercy.
> —1 Peter 2:9-10

Journal about the untruths you believed during childhood and the praise you needed from others. Journal about who you are in Christ today and praise God for it.

_____
_____
_____
_____
_____
_____
_____
_____
_____
_____
_____
_____
_____

WISDOM AND INTUITION

TODAY, WE ARE able to stop the chaotic thoughts inside our head and listen to the soft small voice of God. We can relax, listen, and apply our intelligent side to make positive decisions for our life. We have gained wisdom from experience and have learned to not make life-changing decisions whenever we're in emotional turmoil.

As children we were taught to obey our elders. Our parents fostered dependence or they often did things for us that we could have done ourselves. That dependence stunted our growth. It might have been difficult for our parents to watch us make mistakes. They might have felt our mistakes reflected on them because others might think they were not good parents. Today, we can make mistakes, learn, and be happy. Today, we can use the intuition and wisdom God gave us.

We have learned from poor decisions and mistakes that caused pain. We now trust the inner voice and the Word of God to prompt us to make positive decisions and to avoid destructive ones.

Today, we run the race of life as a runner would run a race to win. We can take one day at a time and not grow weary.

FROM GOD'S HEART TO MINE

Do you not know that in a race all the runners run, but only one gets the prize? Run in such a way as to get the prize. Everyone who competes in the games goes into strict training. They do it to get a crown that will not last; but we do it to get a crown that will last forever.
—1 Corinthians 9:24-25

Therefore, since we are surrounded by such a great cloud of witnesses, let us throw off everything that hinders and the sin that so easily entangles, and let us run with perseverance the race marked out for us. Let us fix our eyes on Jesus, the author and perfector of our faith, who for the joy set before him endured the cross, scorning its shame, and sat down at the right hand of the throne of God.
—Hebrews 12:1-2

I guide you in the way of wisdom and lead you along straight paths. When you walk, your steps will not be hampered; when you run, you will not stumble. Hold on to instruction; do not let it go; guard it well for it is your life. Do not set foot on the path of the wicked or walk in the way of evil men. Avoid it, do not travel on it; turn from it and go on your way.
—Proverbs 4:11-15

Journal about the paths you took in life that hampered your steps and kept you from running the race that God set for you.

Journal about a time when you took the steps God would have you take.

_____
_____
_____
_____
_____
_____

ANGER

WHEN WE WERE children we often got hurt; we either blew up and threw temper tantrums or turned our emotional woundedness inward on ourselves. We often felt disrespected or belittled by others' treatment. Anger was a way to ward off the pain but it pushed others away and kept us lonely. It destroyed any communication so we were unable to solve the problem or bring up resolutions for fear of another blow up. We would feel guilty for yelling unkind things at others and damage ourselves with unkind self-talk. This sometimes led to withdrawal and depression.

Our parents were the models for how we dealt with emotions. Anger was used to relieve their frustration while spewing forth criticism and rage. We learned to stuff feelings of anger, only to explode like a volcano whenever the pain grew unbearable. We would feel as if we were stuck between a terrible two-year-old and a rebellious teenager. Today, we will no longer allow our parents' or others' behaviors to be our example or allow the angry rebellious child or teenager within to control our lives. Today, Christ will be our model and Scripture will be the guide for our behavior.

Today, we will be proactive and discuss problems rather than be a reactor. Today, if we feel hurt or anger, we will take responsibility for our own behavior and talk about our feelings instead of blowing up.

FROM GOD'S HEART TO MINE

'In your anger do not sin': Do not let the sun go down while you are still angry, and do not give the devil a foothold… Get rid of all bitterness, rage and anger, brawling and slander, along with every form of malice. Be kind and compassionate to one another, forgiving each other, just as in Christ God forgave you.
—Ephesians 4:26-27, 31-32

'But I tell you, do not resist an evil person. If someone strikes you on the right cheek, turn to him the other.'
—Matthew 5:39

Jesus said to turn the other cheek. He said this so we would not be reactors to others' sin. We then become responsible to God for our actions. We are not responsible for other peoples' actions—only our own—so not becoming a reactor allows God to be there for us in tough situations. No matter what situation we are in, it is never okay to sin. Today we understand that God wants us to take responsibility for our own behavior. What others do or think is not important, but our character is of utmost importance to God. We can feel stronger as we no longer let the sun go down on our anger. Whenever possible, we work out solutions to whatever problems arise. We do not run from hurt, but embrace it and work it out with God and others whenever possible.

Journal about how the next time someone hurts you, you will walk away, and then whenever possible, come back later and talk it out, do something nice, or just go to God for help to forgive and get over the pain.

_____

_____

_____

_____

LOSS

TODAY WITH GOD, we are able to ride the waves of life and understand emotions because we have experience and Someone by our side that designed us to feel emotions. Losing a loved one is a painful process. The pain is unbearable and we would do anything to avoid it. We were taught by observation and discussions from others to keep busy, get out, go shopping, eat, take pills, a drink, or run to a man or woman just to get away from the pain. It's never okay to sin no matter how much pain we are in.

Today, we have learned to not run from our feelings. We can feel them and do not run because we understand our emotions and the process when we lose someone we love.

At first there is a period of shock that God allows to help us stabilize until the reality hits. There are times when waves of pain come over us and we feel as though we will drown in the overwhelming feelings of loss. We go to sleep in tears and wake with a sense that this is all a bad dream. We cry out to Jesus. His words can permeate our soul. At times we feel guilty that we didn't do enough to prevent the situation, or maybe we didn't tell them we loved them enough. We don't need to carry the guilt along with the loss; we are forgiven for whatever sin we might have committed.

FROM GOD'S HEART TO MINE

> Blessed are those who mourn for they will be comforted.
> —Matthew 5:4

Where is the comfort? We only feel pain. We ache to our bones with grief. Sorrow hangs over us like a cloud. We can no longer enjoy the simple pleasures of a child's laughter, or the beauty of a flower. We feel as if we're in a desert standing on shifting sand. We cry out to God, "Where are You? I know You are here. You understand the loss. You hear my cries, You know my tears are many." Today, we will allow the Lord to comfort us. We know how He loves us, His children, and that He gave His only begotten Son to die for us because of that love. He knows the pain of losing His Son for a time.

Today, we wait on the Lord.

> I wait patiently for the LORD; he turned to me and heard my cry. He lifted me out of the slimy pit, out of the mud and mire; he set my feet on a rock and gave me a firm place to stand. He put a new song in my mouth, a hymn of praise to our God... Blessed is the man who makes the LORD his trust.
> —Psalm 40:1-4

We will trust the Lord to hang on to us through this time. As we turn toward Him, we feel ourselves growing stronger each day. Our hope is in the Lord.

> You are my help and my deliverer; O my God, do not delay.
> —Psalm 40:17

Today, we absorb God's love for us and take special care of ourselves. We focus on those people who love us. We surround ourselves with friends and family who are caring and loving and who will allow us to grieve until we are done. It is not on their timing, but when the process is over for us. We will not wallow in pity, but take the time to cry each

LOSS

day and then do what we need to do. When we are tired, we will rest. We can take hold of God and stand again. He is our rock and He will never leave us or forsake us. He, the Holy Spirit, is here with us.

> The Lord is my rock, my fortress and my deliverer; my God is my rock, in whom I take refuge, my shield and the horn of my salvation. He is my stronghold, my refuge and my savior—from violent men you save me. ⁴I call to the Lord, who is worthy of praise, and I am saved from my enemies.
> —2 Samuel 22:2-4

Journal about the losses in your life and call on the Lord to heal the pain of loss.

_____
_____
_____
_____
_____
_____
_____
_____
_____
_____
_____
_____
_____

HURT, HEALING, AND TRUST

TENSION PERMEATES OUR soul when in the dark of night unhealed wounds well up inside. We struggle to push down the pain. We have tried to cover pain with busyness, obsessions, people, and things, but the pain always returns. The child within has so much pain, yet all that is needed is for someone to listen, acknowledge, and understand.

Today, we can talk to God and know He listens and embraces the pain of His child. We can trust God to keep us safe. We can be reassured and trust that God understands the pain and hurt as no one else can. We can visualize the child safe in His arms. We can see ourselves crying as God wipes away the tears. We feel the deep understanding from God's heart.

Today, we can connect with and understand how people have betrayed, beaten, and defamed Jesus. We relate to how people blamed Him for things He did not do. We relate to how people rejected His love and turned away. We have all experienced those things, but we see that God has endured the pain of generations, for the world and for us. Our broken heart is healed in Christ's understanding and love.

FROM GOD'S HEART TO MINE

He heals the brokenhearted and binds up their wounds. He determines the number of the stars and calls them each by name. Great is our Lord and mighty in power; his understanding has no limit.
—Psalm 147:3-5

Journal about how you have been hurt and how God is there for you.

_____
_____
_____
_____
_____
_____
_____
_____
_____
_____
_____
_____
_____
_____
_____
_____
_____
_____

DISAPPOINTMENTS

SO MANY TIMES we have given love, attention, and time to another only to be left empty. We loved our parents, relatives, and friends, and we had expectations they would return the love. We were naive children, not understanding the social world. We were disappointed when we discovered that in giving love, it was not always returned. We would feel disappointed, depleted, hurt, and hopeless. At some point, the child within gave up trying to love. But now we have discovered that Christ's love does not disappoint us! He is always there and will never leave us or forsake us.

Today, we understand that others look at the outward appearance and can be mean. There are many times when jealousy, prejudices, and greed override love and kindness. What the world thinks is beautiful is not something God considers.

God looks at the heart of man, not his outward appearance. When the prophet Samuel was instructed by God to anoint a new king for Israel He sent him to the house of a man named Jesse. When Jesse brought his first son to Samuel, God rejected Eliab, as the next king even though Samuel thought surely this would be God's choice. It was then that God said to Samuel, "Do not consider his appearance or his height, for I have rejected him. The Lord does not look at the things man looks at. Man looks at the outward appearance, but the Lord looks at the heart" (1 Samuel 16:7).

Today, we are set free in Christ. We can trust God's love for us. We can love God, others, and ourselves without expecting anything in return. We can allow God's love to overflow to others because of His love for us.

> Therefore, since we have been justified through faith, we have peace with God through our Lord Jesus Christ, through whom we have gained access by faith into this grace in which we now stand. And we rejoice in the hope of the glory of God. Not only so, but we can also rejoice in our sufferings, because we know that suffering produces perseverance; perseverance, character; and character, hope. And hope does not disappoint us, because God has poured out his love into our hearts by the Holy Spirit, whom he has given us.
>
> —Romans 5:1-5

Journal about disappointments and the love of God.

_____
_____
_____
_____
_____
_____
_____
_____
_____

LOVE

For love is from God.

—John 4:7

God is love. Whoever lives in love lives in God, and God in him.
—1 John 4:16

LOVE IS WHAT infants need to survive. As an adult, we have substituted worldly things and addictions to help fill our empty hearts. We are left with emptiness because of inadequate parents, friends, and relatives who showed little love, compassion, understanding, or encouragement towards us as children.

> Love is patient, love is kind. It does not envy, it does not boast, it is not proud. It is not rude, it is not self-seeking, it is not easily angered, and it keeps no record of wrongs. Love does not delight in evil but rejoices with the truth. It always protects, always trusts, always hopes, and always perseveres.
> —1 Corinthians 13:4-7

FROM GOD'S HEART TO MINE

Today, we can provide love, compassion, and encouragement to the child within. We can open our hearts and take in the love that God has provided for us daily. We can see God's love in the face of a child, the beauty of the sky, and little creatures. We can hear the giggle of a baby, the sound of a croaking frog, and the chirping of birds and absorb God's love. We can now feel love in a healthy touch from others. We can feel love and energy from smiling faces. We realize love is available in a variety of forms. Today, we will watch for and feel the overflowing love of God.

Journal about all the loving things God has in the world just for our amusement, beauty, or comfort. Look at the bugs, flowers, sky, and find God's love in the small things. We can feel the love of God in the laughter of children, and learn to laugh and play and experience the adventure of life before us, no matter what life brings. Talk to your child within about how much God loves you.

_____

_____

_____

_____

_____

_____

_____

_____

_____

_____

_____

_____

COUNSEL

Listen to counsel and accept discipline, that you may be wise the rest of your days. Many are the plans in a man's heart, but the counsel of the LORD will stand. What is desirable in a man is his kindness, and it is better to be a poor man than a liar. The fear of the LORD leads to life, so that one may sleep satisfied, untouched by evil.

—Proverbs 19:20-23 (NASB)

Where there is no guidance the people fall, but in abundance of counselors there is victory.

—Proverbs 11:14 (NASB)

AS A CHILD, there was no guidance, only yelling and criticism. We had no one to model healthy emotional strength. We had to make our own way and rules. We made painful mistakes and learned from them, but we had no idea how to live a healthy life. We reacted to the people around us. If they said we were bad, we must be bad. Today, we know that we needed to be taught by trustworthy people who cared enough to guide us into who God made us to be.

Today, we can model our lives after the principles in the Word of God. We can model our lives after Christ's. We know we do not have to be perfect and can grow up into the person God intended us to be. Today, our behaviors and our direction are focused on moving toward righteousness.

We can accept help; we have the freedom to listen to others who have taken the path of righteousness. We trust the Word of God. We can filter information from others through the Word of God and trust our life will improve.

Today, we no longer have to go through life alone, withdrawn, or isolated to stay safe. We have God, mentors, and trusted adults to guide our growth. We know it is still our choice which direction we choose, but are no longer alone because God and His Spirit are with us forever.

Journal

EXPECTATIONS

DISTORTED, UNREAL EXPECTATIONS create misery by setting others and us up for failure. As a child, we set up a fantasy world to be able to tolerate a chaotic home. We loved everyone and expected everyone to love us back. We thought that God wanted us to love everyone. Yes, we are to love others, but without expectations of them loving us back. We would feel rejected, abandoned, or unloved when others didn't live up to our expectations. What we didn't understand is that when we live by impossible expectations or distorted fantasies about people, we get disappointed. Do we expect that others should always understand our feelings and not misperceive our intentions? Do we expect that we should never feel lonely or unloved, even in relationships?

Today, we can view situations more realistically when we are grounded in God's Word. We can understand that impossible expectations set us up for disappointment in others and ourselves.

Today, we receive true love from God, and when we receive love and caring from others, that's icing on the cake. Today, we have the courage to go on because we no longer have to try to live up to others' impossible expectations and feel shamed. We can eagerly expect God to work in our lives as we read the Word and apply it. We don't have to expect others to fulfill our expectations; they are who they are and God has them in His hand.

Today, we can let go and let God. We can expect God to be who He says He is and do what He says He will do, knowing that He always has our best interests at heart.

Today, we can recognize that when we say, "I should," we are setting up unrealistic expectations. The "shoulds" are rigid and bind us. Today, we will change the "shoulds" to prayers for God's will in our lives and accept the path He has for us.

> I eagerly expect and hope that I will in no way be ashamed, but will have sufficient courage so that now as always Christ will be exalted in my body, whether by life or by death. For to me, to live is Christ and to die is gain.
> —Philippians 1:20-21

> Jesus said, 'If you hold to my teaching, you are really my disciples. Then you will know the truth, and the truth will set you free.'
> —John 8:31-32

God is the Spirit of Truth, and the truth shall set you free. Today, we are free from destructive unrealistic expectations and can view life realistically. We are free to live our lives with the gifts we have been given without expectations that drain our creativity and joy.

Journal about your impossible expectations and turn them into what is the truth.

_____
_____
_____
_____

EMOTIONS

IN OUR DYSFUNCTIONAL families there were no boundaries. Everyone had to walk around on eggshells, because we never knew when our parents would blow up. Our parents made us feel we were the problem. We were made to feel that emotions were bad or that we would make things worse if we talked about our feelings. We had to pretend to be happy all the time. We felt that if we were just good enough we could make our parents happy. This is when we began to rescue them emotionally. Did we have to block emotions and stop feelings in chaotic or painful situations?

Today, we realize we are not the reason for other peoples' emotional discomfort. We realize the source of their emotional pain is inside them and we also realize that we can do nothing to take away that emotional pain. We do know we can support and encourage others who are having a difficult time. Today, we know we do not have to change ourselves to make others happy. We can't save them from their inner self. We know we have to "let go" and "let God work" with them. Only God can save them from their own self-destructive mood-driven patterns of living. God made emotions and He expects us to feel all of them. He offers His love and comfort during those times if we ask Him for help and then accept it. Similarly, we can mourn and comfort others, but we don't have to save them from these emotions and pretend they don't exist. To feel when things are painful takes courage. When we cut off feelings we cut ourselves off from the joy of life as well as the pain. We have a God who understands the pain. God wants us to be whole and present in life, not in denial, because He can't deliver us in denial.

When someone loses a child, gets cancer, or has marital or children problems, we can pray with them and for them and encourage them as God does for us. We have our perfect role model in Christ. We no longer have to anesthetize our lives. Instead we can allow emotions to enrich our lives and our spirits. We can recognize how valuable emotions are and that they are a gift from God that we can accept with gratefulness.

> Blessed are the poor in spirit, for theirs is the kingdom of heaven. Blessed are those who mourn, for they will be comforted. Blessed are the meek, for they will inherit the earth. Blessed are those who hunger and thirst for righteousness, for they will be filled. Blessed are the merciful, for they will be shown mercy. Blessed are the pure in heart, for they will see God. Blessed are the peacemakers, for they will be called sons of God. Blessed are those who are persecuted because of righteousness, for theirs is the kingdom of heaven. Blessed are you when people insult you, persecute you and falsely say all kinds of evil against you because of me. Rejoice and be glad, because great is your reward in heaven, for in the same way they persecuted the prophets who were before you.
>
> —Matthew 5:3-12

We take on the heart of God when we can mourn with those who mourn, etc. Today, we understand God gave us emotions and He is the one who knows best how to handle them. There is much pain when we sin against God. But sometimes others suffer for our sin, including our children. We are to mourn our sin and make amends whenever possible, without hurting others. David pleaded with God to spare his baby from death, but accepted the harsh consequence. He was a warrior who could not allow the long process of mourning. He needed to acknowledge his pain. He was able to comfort his wife, and they had other children, but it could never erase the sinful act and the child dying. Because we have Christ's forgiveness, we can acknowledge the pain and move on with forgiveness after we have truly repented. David is an example of someone who experienced the pain of his sin and how it affected his family and other families. Others tried to soften the blow, but there was no way to soften the death of his child. The pain of our sin often produces consequences for our innocent children, family, or friends. David mourned.

> After Nathan had gone home, the LORD struck the child that Uriah's wife had borne to David, and he became ill. David pleaded with God for the child. He fasted and went into his house and spent the nights lying on the ground. The elders of his household stood beside him to get him up from the ground, but he refused, and he would not eat any food with them. On the seventh day the child died. David's servants were afraid to tell him that the child was dead, for they thought, 'While the child was still living, we spoke to David but he would not listen to us. How can we tell him the child is dead? He may do something desperate.' David noticed that his servants were whispering among themselves and he realized the child was dead. 'Is the child dead?' he asked. 'Yes,' they replied, 'he is dead.' Then David got up from the ground. After he had washed, put on lotions and changed his clothes, he went into the house of the LORD and worshiped. Then he went to his own house, and at his request they served him food, and he ate. His servants asked him, 'Why are you acting this way? While the child was alive, you fasted and wept, but now that the child is dead, you get up and eat!' He answered, 'While the child was still alive, I fasted and wept. I thought, "Who knows? The Lord may be gracious to me and let the child live." But now that he is dead, why should I fast? Can I bring him back again? I will go to him, but he will not return to me.' Then David comforted his wife Bathsheba, and he went to her and

FROM GOD'S HEART TO MINE

lay with her. She gave birth to a son, and they named him Solomon. The Lord loved him.

—2 Samuel 12:15-24

There is a time to mourn and a time for joy. From despair to elation, God is always with us. He doesn't always take us out of the pain, but He sits with us in it. Today, we can choose to take on the attributes of God's healthy attitude concerning emotional maturity. Today, we can set boundaries and "let Go and let God" while honoring another's pain and our own.

Journal about fears you have concerning emotions. Journal about the valuable resource and gift emotions can be.

_____
_____
_____
_____
_____
_____
_____
_____
_____
_____
_____

GENDER

TODAY, WE CAN accept our God-given gender as a gift. When we are children, some families elevate the status of one gender over another. Having boys to some is an honor, while having a girl was just having a girl. The messages were spoken or unspoken but we understood that we were less. We learned to get attention in either negative or positive ways. We are cute when we are young but those same behaviors do not work when we are older. We can feel neglected or criticized, inferior because we are a boy or girl. We act as if we are equal. We try to be good students and we work hard at being good. At times we just want to cry and give up because it is so hard to please others.

The messages were damaging to our hearts and souls. We would try to engage with others and get rejected. We would withdraw and isolate, and we became very empty.

Today, we can acknowledge the beauty that God gave us on the inside and the outside. We are all made in His image with a nurturing and loving heart. He made women beautiful and unique as the flowers. He made men with different strengths. He makes us all strong through trials. We understand the world degrades the inner and outer beauty of women today. By trying to be a perfect beauty or a good-looking jock, we were working to get unhealthy attention. We were trying to meet the world's expectations of a beautiful woman or good-looking man.

Today, we realize we could never live up to the expectations of the world. Today, we embrace the women/men we are. We can be caring, nurturing, financially responsible, educated, and have an opinion without feeling inferior. Today, we can look at ourselves in the mirror and see the beauty God has given us in our eyes, body, and soul. We all have God-given gifts and we can explore what those are. We have freedom to become who God made us to be.

> You are all sons of God through faith in Christ Jesus, for all of you who were baptized into Christ have clothed yourselves with Christ. There is neither Jew nor Greek, slave nor free, *male nor female,* for *you are all one* in Christ Jesus. If you belong to Christ, then you are Abraham's seed, and heirs according to the promise.
> —Galatians 3:26-29

Journal your experiences as a female/male.

_____
_____
_____
_____
_____
_____
_____
_____
_____
_____

CONFUSION

CONFUSION CAUSES A fog to hang over our days. It permeates our thoughts, feelings, and desires. It causes us to become anxious, to procrastinate, and to become paralyzed.

Chaos and confusion are not from God. Chaos and confusion happen every day in many dysfunctional homes. It makes a home a place where it is difficult to trust. Parents could demand a specific behavior while modeling the opposite. They would tell us what to think or feel instead of understanding what we might be feeling.

Today, we can learn to identify our own needs and embrace our own feelings. We no longer feel the cloud of confusion, but can walk the path before us with clarity and peace. We can walk in peace because we know the God who goes before us lights our path when we are in His will.

> Your word is a lamp to my feet and a light for my path. I have taken an oath and confirmed it, that I will follow your righteous laws.
> —Psalm 119:105-106

God is our model today and He is not a God of chaos but gives us direction and purpose. Obstacles are no longer a threat but a way for

FROM GOD'S HEART TO MINE

God to help us develop perseverance and strength. They allow us to see how God is there and our life becomes a testimony for His glory.

> Consider it pure joy, my brothers, whenever you face trials of many kinds, because you know that the testing of your faith develops perseverance. Perseverance must finish its work so that you may be mature and complete, not lacking anything.
> —James 1:2-4

Journal your thoughts about yourself and your life.

_____
_____
_____
_____
_____
_____
_____
_____
_____
_____
_____
_____
_____
_____
_____
_____

GUILTY AS JUDGED

AS CHILDREN WE often felt judged. We never felt we could be good enough. We were criticized or hit when we didn't even know what we did wrong. Critical parenting caused us to become critical of ourselves. As the years went by we began to put ourselves on trial daily, feeling self-disapproval. We could never be pretty/handsome enough, intelligent enough, or nice enough. Feeling bad about ourselves was a constant condition. Today as Christians, we can fall into the error of believing we have to be as perfect as Christ. When we fail we might feel guilty or sad and this can become a circular pattern. We do something wrong and feel constant guilt that we can never be good enough, just like when we were children. Then we criticize ourselves again. Criticism becomes instant in our heads. We feel we have to accept that we are just innately bad. Sometimes the only attention we get is negative attention and it is better than no attention at all. Each criticism creates a greater need to be praised. We need to feel we have worth. We need to be loved unconditionally. We never feel we have any value and depression becomes a way of life.

The guilt created a wall that only God's love could permeate. Even though we know we were loved, we never felt it. The wall took years to build, and with God we are in the process of learning to trust and be vulnerable again because God's love is unconditional. He knows our inadequacies. In the growth process we have to realize that we have a wall, trust God, and accept His love. We can then begin to believe we are lovable and remove the wall, brick by brick, with God's help. We could accept we were bad, rejecting anything good about ourselves. We could often be manipulated with praise from others because we were in such need of human acceptance and affirmation. We realized we could be sweet talked into doing things we really did not want to do, just for a little adoration or praise. The praise worked, but it was fleeting and empty.

Today, we can treat ourselves in a loving manner because when we confess our sins He is faithful to forgive them. All our sins are washed away and thrown as far as the east is from the west.

Today, we understand healthy guilt is there to guide us into doing the right thing before God. Toxic guilt is damaging and can turn anger inward or outward. Healthy guilt guides us into truth and asking for forgiveness to sanctify us. This is love.

> For as a high as the heavens are above the earth, so great is his love for those who fear him; as far as the east is from the west, so far has he removed our transgressions from us.
> —Psalm 103:11-12

> ...who forgives all your sins and heals all your diseases; who redeems your life from the pit and crowns you with love and compassion, who satisfies your desires with good things so that your youth is renewed like the eagle's. The LORD works righteousness and justice for all the oppressed.
> —Psalm 103:3-6

Today, we can allow the Word to sink into our hearts along with the love of God. We realize the praise we received from others was not love. It was nice and felt good for a moment. *Approval is earned;*

GUILTY AS JUDGED

love is unconditional. Jesus died for us even when we were yet sinners. He died so we might be freed from the bondage of sin and the sin of criticizing ourselves. We have been set free from the old self. It is our loving Father who is teaching us to be comfortable as His children and walk in righteousness. Greater is He who is in us than he who is in the world. The Spirit in us is there for our sanctification and to strengthen us in Christ.

Journal about your personal experience of being set free.

_____
_____
_____
_____
_____
_____
_____
_____
_____
_____
_____
_____
_____
_____
_____
_____

SECURITY

AS CHILDREN FROM dysfunctional families, we were plagued with insecurities, fears, and needs, and we became caretakers of our parents. We tried to fulfill their needs, but we were the ones who needed to be taken care of and loved. We became empty children as the family depleted what little resources we had. We often felt overwhelmed. We realize today that we took care of our parents' emotional needs and became the perfect child out of survival, or we became the rebellious child to get away. We could not handle the chaos and confusion, but we could go into our own world of rebellion, or take the path of perfection. Getting out of the house or isolating by reading, doing homework, sitting at the computer, or talking to friends helped to separate us from the household's chaotic environment. This soon became a habit that felt very comfortable. We could be rebellious and it felt good for a time, but the consequences were painful. Whenever we felt overwhelmed we could retreat to the cave away from friends or family. At times, it was productive and we received much praise for achievements. We tried to be perfect to give ourselves a sense of security and control. Control was the key to feeling security that the child needed to help the family stabilize.

FROM GOD'S HEART TO MINE

As an adult, we can often feel ourselves falling into old patterns and traps. When we feel things are out of control and we have to be perfect or rebel, we can talk to God and stand on His promises. He is our security, our rock, and we can trust in Him. We are promised that He will not give us more than we can handle. We can hang onto the promise that He will work all things together for good for those who love Him and purpose to do His will. With the promises of God we can humble ourselves, let go, and allow God to do the work. Today, we can find peace in our soul because Jesus is a safe place to land. Christ's love is never interrupted, withdrawn, or revoked because of anything we can or can't do. We then can re-engage with others and live in God's security.

> The LORD is my rock, my fortress and my deliverer; my God is my rock, in whom I take refuge. He is my shield and the horn [strength] of my salvation, I call to the LORD, who is worthy of praise, and I am saved from my enemies.
> —Psalm 18:2-3

> As for God, his way is perfect; the word of the LORD is flawless. He is a shield for all who take refuge in him. For who is God besides the Lord? And who is the Rock except our God? It is God who arms me with strength and makes my way perfect. He makes my feet like the feet of a deer; he enables me to stand on the heights... You broaden the path beneath me, so my ankles do not turn.
> —Psalm 18:30-33, 36

Journal about your insecurities, fears, or feeling overwhelmed and pray and ask the Lord to help you feel secure in His love.

_____
_____
_____
_____

MATURITY

AS A CHILD we were abused, and because of the abuse, our emotional growth was stunted. We were never allowed to make mistakes without feeling guilty. Everything we were taught was accompanied with a great deal of screaming or shaming. We might have felt we had to be perfect and couldn't. We craved love and praise from others and when we didn't get it, we searched and indulged ourselves in worldly gratifications to make ourselves feel good.

Today, we realize children are characteristically in a constant learning process and making mistakes is a part of that process. Children are dependent on caretakers to teach them the social world and survival. Children are born vulnerable and caretakers are put there by God to protect, teach, and guide them into maturity. Today, we do not accept the shame or guilt of the child who was just learning to be in this world. Today, we can allow ourselves to make mistakes because they are an important part of the learning process.

Today, we no longer have to live as we used to in the futility of our thinking. We no longer harden our hearts because of ignorance. We now can be sensitive to the Spirit and God's leading. We no longer have to give ourselves over to sensuality or indulge in impurity, with a continual lust for more. We no longer have to be tossed back and forth like a child by every teaching from the world. We have put off the old self, which was corrupt and deceived by desire. We can accept God's love, grace, mercy, and forgiveness that heal the soul.

> So I tell you this, and insist on it in the Lord, that you must no longer live as the Gentiles do, in the futility of their thinking. They are darkened in their understanding and separated from the life of God because of the ignorance that is in them due to the hardening of their hearts. Having lost all sensitivity, they have given themselves over to sensuality so as to indulge in every kind of impurity, with a continual lust for more.
> —Ephesians 4:17-10

Today, we can give ourselves time to learn the Word and apply it to our lives daily. We do not have to be critical when we make mistakes. We can forgive ourselves because when we ask Jesus to forgive us we are forgiven. We can confess our mistakes and think about how we can do it differently the next time. We have help from the Holy Spirit. We know we are a work in progress, not perfect. Only God is perfect. We can pray for forgiveness and guidance to keep us from willfully sinning as we keep our eyes on the Lord.

In Ephesians, *maturity* is described as living the life worthy of the calling you have received, making every effort to keep the unity of the Spirit through the bond of peace. It is God who is preparing His people for works of service so the body of Christ is built up, and this includes you.

> …until we reach unity in the faith and in the knowledge of the Son of God and become mature, attaining to the whole measure of the fullness of Christ. Then we will no longer be infants, tossed back and forth by the waves, and blown here and there by every wind of teaching and by the cunning and craftiness of men in their deceitful scheming. Instead, speaking the truth in love, we will in all things grow up into him who is the Head, that is, Christ.
> —Ephesians 4:13-15

MATURITY

Consider it pure joy, my brothers, whenever you face trials of many kinds, because you know that the testing of your faith develops perseverance. Perseverance must finish its work so that you may be mature and complete, not lacking anything. If any of you lacks wisdom, he should ask God, who gives generously to all without finding fault, and it will be given to him. But when he asks, he must believe and not doubt, because he who doubts is like a wave of the sea, blown and tossed by the wind."
—James 1:2-6

The law of the LORD is perfect, reviving the soul. The statutes of the LORD are trustworthy, making wise the simple. The precepts of the LORD are right, giving joy to the heart. The commands of the LORD are radiant, giving light to the eyes… Who can discern his errors? Forgive my hidden faults. Keep your servant also from willful sins; may they not rule over me. Then will I be blameless, innocent of great transgression.
—Psalm 18:7-8, 12-13

Journal about how you are increasing in maturity.

_____
_____
_____
_____
_____
_____
_____
_____

GOD'S PURPOSE FOR MY LIFE

AS CHILDREN WE did not know why we were born. We could not contemplate the wonders of the world. We felt lost at times because we only understood who we were because of what others told us. We were taught that we could be anything we wanted to be, but life soon confused that message. We soon found that there were barriers because of gender, looks, status, or level of education. We started out as children excited and loving to learn. The critical adults who could not handle the energy of the adventuresome child soon hindered the excitement. Often other children would put us down to make themselves look better.

Today, we are excited in Christ. We have a purpose for our lives as we use the gifts that God gave us for His purpose. We no longer have to be confused or tossed back and forth by what others think or by their scheming to make themselves look better. Christ's love has given us back the child who loves to explore and learn.

> It was he who gave some to be apostles, some to be prophets, some to be evangelists, and some to be pastors and teachers, to prepare God's people for works of service, so that the body of Christ may be built up until we all reach unity in the faith and in the knowledge of the

FROM GOD'S HEART TO MINE

Son of God and become mature, attaining to the whole measure of the fullness of Christ. Then we will no longer be infants, tossed back and forth by the waves, and blown here and there by every wind of teaching and by the cunning and craftiness of men in their deceitful scheming. Instead, speaking the truth in love, we will in all things grow up into him who is the Head, that is Christ.
—Ephesians 4:11-15

Journal about your gifts and what might be your purpose in Christ.

_____
_____
_____
_____
_____
_____
_____
_____
_____
_____
_____
_____
_____
_____
_____
_____
_____

CHANGE AND SADNESS

AS WE AGE, we often contemplate the changes of life. Sometimes these changes create a sadness that permeates the soul. For instance, we are the only creatures on this earth that know we are dying. Our understanding of how short life is increases each time we see a death of a TV personality, extended family, or close family and friends. Many just deny or pretend to be having fun when they are truly in pain.

It is difficult to learn to let go each day of things we cherish. Looking at the past we are sad because we no longer have the experience of finding our first real love. We no longer can experience the excitement of getting married. We can never repeat the joy of having our first newborn baby; watching them take their first step; becoming a toddler; then a little girl/boy; and eventually becoming a young woman/man and possibly a parent. The hardest of all is the parent having to let go of the adult child. Looking ahead is difficult because most of life's dreams have happened. There is little to look forward to except to watch or help others go through the cycle of life. Unless we have the Lord there is no purpose. God gives us purpose and direction until our last day on earth, and then we have eternity with God, who is perfect and holy. There is a time for everything in life.

There is an appointed time for everything. And there is a time for every event under heaven—

A time to give birth and a time to die;
A time to plant and a time to uproot what is planted.
A time to kill and a time to heal;
A time to tear down and a time to build up.
A time to weep and a time to laugh;
A time to mourn and a time to dance.
A time to throw stones and a time to gather stones;
A time to embrace and a time to shun embracing.
A time to search and a time to give up as lost;
A time to keep and a time to throw away.
A time to tear apart and a time to sew together;
A time to be silent and a time to speak.
A time to love and a time to hate;
A time for war and a time for peace.

—Ecclesiastes 3:1-8

He has made everything appropriate in its time. He has also set eternity in their heart, yet so that man will not find out the work, which God has done from the beginning even to the end. I know that there is nothing better for them than to rejoice and to do good in one's lifetime; moreover, that every man who eats and drinks sees good in all his labor—it is the gift of God.

—Ecclesiastes 3:11-13

The Book of Ecclesiastes describes the futility of endeavor, wisdom, pleasure, possessions, and labor and how God changes the futility to a blessing.

For what does a man get in all his labor and in his striving with which he labors under the sun? Because all his days his task is painful and grievous; even at night his mind does not rest. This too is vanity. There is nothing better for a man than to eat and drink and tell himself that

CHANGE AND SADNESS

his labor is good. This also I have seen that it is from the hand of God. For who can eat and who can have enjoyment without Him? For to a person who is good in His sight He has given wisdom and knowledge and joy, while to the sinner He has given the task of gathering and collecting so that he may give to one who is good in God's sight. This too is vanity and striving after wind.
—Ecclesiastes 2:22-26 (NASB)

Sorrow is better than laughter, for when a face is sad a heart may be happy. The mind of the wise is in the house of mourning, while the mind of fools is in the house of pleasure… In the day of prosperity be happy, but in the day of adversity consider—God made the one as well as the other so that man may not discover anything that will be after him.
—Ecclesiastes 7:3-4, 14 (NASB)

Read more of Ecclesiastes and journal about your sorrows over changes and loss.

_____
_____
_____
_____
_____
_____
_____
_____
_____
_____
_____

SECRETS

THE FAMILY ALWAYS had secrets and we were taught not to let anyone know our business. The family could take care of any problems from within. The pain came because no one took care of anything. Everything was hidden. We all walked around in pain. We often had to go into denial and fantasy to survive. We had to pretend we were the perfect family, while we knew it was rotting our souls. No conflict was ever resolved, no hurt ever soothed or healed. There was only a repeat, over and over, of the same critical spirit from within the family. Having to keep the secrets of abuse and pain took its toll on everyone. Some of the family escaped into drugs or alcohol, others into relationships, and others tried to do the opposite and become perfect. Nothing worked. It was a sick family system that perpetuated sin.

Today, we are set free. We have nothing to hide, because we are forgiven. We can confess our sins and Jesus is faithful to forgive them. The Bible says in James 5:16, "Therefore confess your sins to each other and pray for each other so that you may be healed. The prayer of a righteous man is powerful and effective." We can feel the release when we confess to the Lord, a counselor, or a trusted friend because God can't deliver us when we are in denial. We no longer have to lie to ourselves. We no longer have to pretend. We need to be taught righteousness so we might become healthy. Thank You, Lord, that You are in the process of helping me become emotionally healthy.

This Psalm says it all:

> Blessed is he whose transgressions are forgiven, whose sins are covered. Blessed is the man whose sin the LORD does not count against him and in whose spirit is no deceit. When I kept silent, my bones wasted away through my groaning all day long. For day and night your hand was heavy upon me; my strength was sapped as in the heat of summer. Then I acknowledged my sin to you and did not cover up my iniquity. I said, 'I will confess my transgressions to the LORD'—and you forgave the guilt of my sin. Therefore let everyone who is godly pray to you while you may be found; surely when the mighty waters rise, they will not reach him. You are my hiding place; you will protect me from trouble and surround me with songs of deliverance. I will instruct you and teach you in the way you should go; I will counsel you and watch over you. Do not be like the horse or the mule, which have no understanding but must be controlled by bit and the bridle or they will not come to you. Many are the woes of the wicked, but the LORD's unfailing love surrounds the man who trusts in him. Rejoice in the LORD and be glad, you righteous; sing, all you who are upright in heart!
>
> —Psalm 32:1-11

> If we claim to be without sin, we deceive ourselves and the truth is not in us. If we confess our sins, he is faithful and just and will forgive us our sins and purify us from all unrighteousness.
>
> —1 John 1:9-9

Journal about your sin and be truthful to yourself and God. The fourth step of AA is to write an inventory of your defects and strengths and whenever possible, when it would not hurt another, make amends for

SECRETS

those sins. Try this with a pastor or counselor you trust and whom you can be accountable to.

FAILURE

FAILURE IS NOT something that we want to experience. Failure means loss. Fear of failure may cause us to work ourselves to exhaustion so as not to fail. We soon begin to procrastinate out of fear that we can't do something right. We keep putting things off until we begin to feel paralyzed. The worry paralyzes us and we often just give up because it is overwhelming.

When we worry about everything, including what we look like or did we say the right thing, it is often about fear of what others think of us. We turn everything into, "What if they don't like me?" or "What if I just can't do it right?" The failures are in our minds and we have turned everything into a catastrophe if we don't perform to perfection.

Today, we know that if we don't try we have already failed. Trial and error is a part of life that helps us find out what we are good at. Failure helps us learn to do it better the next time or find a different way to succeed. Failure is about learning, practicing, and redoing. We are learning to take one day at a time. We can now pray and ask for God's guidance, and trust in His Word that He is with us always. We are all in process and not perfect. Only God is perfect.

FROM GOD'S HEART TO MINE

Cast all your cares on the Lord and he will sustain you; he will never let the righteous fall.
—Psalm 55:22

'So do not worry, saying, "What shall we eat" or "What shall we drink?" or "What shall we wear?" For the pagans run after all these things, and your heavenly Father knows that you need them. But seek first his kingdom and his righteousness, and all these things will be given to you as well. Therefore do not worry about tomorrow, for tomorrow will worry about itself. Each day has enough trouble of its own.'
—Matthew 6:31-34

Today, we understand that we were made to succeed at what we are good at. We can't be good at everything. We need to find the gifts that God gave us and use those gifts to our potential. Today, we will stop measuring ourselves according to others, but understand who we are and our abilities. Each day we can do our best for the Lord. We can't change the future or the past—we can only do what we can do today. We can begin taking one day at a time because each day has enough in it.

Journal about fear of failure and how it has caused you anxiety and stress. Write, pray, and ask God to reveal the gifts He gave you and thank Him for them.

_____
_____
_____
_____
_____
_____

LIES WE LIVED/CHANGING CHILDLIKE PERSPECTIVES

INNOCENT CHILDREN OFTEN endure painful scenes produced like a movie in their minds by parents who were not aware or didn't care about the damage they were causing. We have all been called cruel names that created devastating emotional wounds and distorted our perspective of ourselves.

Today, we no longer have to live under the lies we believed about ourselves. We can see ourselves as children of God, children of a King, and override the pain caused by the lies. The lies went deep into the depths of our souls and created negative feelings. We can view and bring the ugly scenes into the light of truth with a new perspective. We no longer have to attach painful names to our identity. We have an identity that God gave us. We are lovable, beautiful, capable, and wonderfully made.

Today, we see our past from the perspective of an adult who understands how miserable and unhappy other people were and how they unconsciously wanted us to experience the misery they felt. It worked for a time, but today we can choose to no longer be a victim of others' distorted perspectives of us.

We are more than anyone could ever see or know and God loves us. No one can change us into who they believe we are. When we sin, we have a Savior who understands and forgives us so we can learn from our mistakes. Today, people can't define us by who they think we are or by our mistakes. Today, we have come to an understanding of who God really is. We can't make Him into who we think He is. We have seen people who try to change God into someone they want Him to be, but He can't be anyone but Himself. Thank You, God, for that revelation. God is the "I AM" and He can't be changed. He is the same yesterday, today, and tomorrow. Today we know "I am whom God made me;" no one else is like us and no one can make us into someone we are not.

God's choices are sovereign and we do not have to continue to live under lies and not receive the blessings and gifts that He wants to bestow on His children. He makes us into who He designed us to be.

> Do not be afraid of those who kill the body but cannot kill the soul. Rather, be afraid of the One who can destroy both soul and body in hell. Are not two sparrows sold for a penny? Yet not one of them will fall to the ground apart from the will of your Father. And even the very hairs of your head are all numbered. So don't be afraid; you are worth more than many sparrows.
> —Matthew 10:28-31

> But who are you, O man, to talk back to God? 'Shall what is formed say to him who formed it, "Why did you make me like this?"' Does not the potter have the right to make out of the same lump of clay some pottery for noble purposes and some for common use?
> —Romans 9:20-21

Journal about your distorted perceptions from the past and who you are in Christ now.

_____

_____

_____

CONTROL

WHAT IS CONTROL? Life happens around us and we really have no control. Control is an illusion that makes us feel better. We only have control over our attitudes and ourselves. We have no control over other people, events, or situations. Why is it so important to feel in control? When you come from a life of chaos and traumas, the tendency is to take control because control means security; we feel safe. Today, we can understand that when things feel out of control, we need to let go and we will not be destroyed.

    There is an important lesson to be learned by riding horses. When we tighten the reins on the horse it stops or sometimes fights for freedom. On a mountain path, fear can overtake the rider and he'll want to take control so as to not go over the cliff. Tightening the reins or squeezing the horse with your legs can confuse the horse and create confusion and push it to do the opposite of what you might want. Learning to trust the horse and give it its head and relaxing your body is what is needed. It begins with trusting the horse. The horse does not want to go over the cliff. Trusting the horse is a way to get down the hill safely. Learning to let go allows God to take the reins of our lives.

FROM GOD'S HEART TO MINE

Today, we can realize that when we step in the way, God can't do the work that He needs to do. We can't save other people—sometimes they need to go through the scary times to learn the lessons they need to without us in the way. We can learn to be supportive without taking over for others. Thank You, Lord. What a weight off our shoulders.

> I will give you the keys of the kingdom of heaven; whatever you bind on earth will be bound in heaven, and whatever you loose on earth will be loosed in heaven.
> —Matthew 16:19

> But blessed is the man who trusts in the Lord, whose confidence is in him, He will be like a tree planted by the water that sends out its roots by the stream. It does not fear when the heat comes; its leaves are always green. It has no worries in a year of drought and never fails to bear fruit.
> —Jeremiah 17:7-8

> Come to Me, all who are weary and heavy-laden, and I will give you rest. Take My yoke upon you and learn from Me, for I am gentle and humble in heart, and you shall find rest for your souls. For My yoke is easy and My load is light.
> —Matthew 11:28-30 (NASB)

Journal about control and your feelings about letting go and giving God the reins of your life.

_____

_____

_____

_____

_____

_____

REJECTION

AS A CHILD, we felt rejection when our parents scolded us and we felt we were bad. We felt rejected when others left us out of play or a party. We could feel horrible when others might have laughed at us or called us names. Today, we can link the words and others' actions with self-hatred or self-blame. These are lies we believed about ourselves. We no longer have to believe lies from childhood. Today, we can understand that Jesus came to deal with our sin and imperfections. We can now feel free to accept our own imperfections because as long as we live in this sinful world, our flesh, the world, and Satan's attacks impact us. With Jesus' love these impact us less, because He accepts us and loves us.

Today, we can learn to be less demanding on others and ourselves by realizing no one is perfect; things are not black and white, or all good or all bad because only God is perfect and holy. Instead of feeling rejected and allowing it to turn into self-hatred, we can ask for forgiveness. If we have done something wrong we can remember that God never rejects us as we purpose to do His will. His Son was rejected, betrayed, and killed so we might have eternal life and freedom to choose righteousness and do His will. We are accepted and have a place in the kingdom of God.

FROM GOD'S HEART TO MINE

We are not rejected; we are filled with the Spirit to shed light on the truth of God and reject the lies of darkness so we might be sanctified.

Today, we can feel accepted by God because of what Christ did on the cross. Today, we can enjoy the miracles of being accepted into the kingdom of God, along with the unlimited possibilities he has for us as children of God.

> For God did not send his Son into the world to condemn the world, but to save the world through him.
> —John 3:17

> I will rescue you from your own people and from the Gentiles. I am sending you to them to open their eyes and turn them from darkness to light, and from the power of Satan to God, so that they may receive forgiveness of sins and a place among those who are sanctified by faith in me.
> —Acts 26:17-18

Journal about rejection from the world and acceptance from God.

_____
_____
_____
_____
_____
_____
_____
_____

www.ingramcontent.com/pod-product-compliance
Lightning Source LLC
Chambersburg PA
CBHW030329080526
44584CB00012B/778